The Hardball Handbook

CHRIS MATTHEWS

The Hardball Handbook

Previously published as *Life's a Campaign*

How to Win at Life

RANDOM HOUSE TRADE PAPERBACKS · NEW YORK

2009 Random House Trade Paperback Edition

Copyright © 2007, 2009 by Christopher J. Matthews

Published in the United States by Random House Trade Paperbacks,
an imprint of The Random House Publishing Group,
a division of Random House, Inc., New York.

RANDOM HOUSE TRADE PAPERBACKS and colophon
are trademarks of Random House, Inc.

Originally published in slightly different form and in hardcover as
Life's a Campaign in the United States by Random House, an imprint of The
Random House Publishing Group, a division of Random House, Inc., in 2007.

LIBRARY OF CONGRESS CATALOGING-IN-PUBLICATION DATA
Matthews, Christopher.
The hardball handbook: how to win at life / Chris Matthews.
p.   cm.
Includes index.
ISBN 978-0-8129-7597-0
1. Communication in politics—United States. 2. Politicians—United States—
Psychology. 3. Political campaigns—United States. 4. Political psychology.
5. Persuasion (Psychology). 6. Matthews, Christopher, 1945– I. Title.
JA85.2.U6M38 2007
324.70973—dc22   2007023219

Printed in the United States of America

www.atrandom.com

2 4 6 8 9 7 5 3

Book design by Carole Lowenstein

To my brothers,
Herb, Jim, Bruce,
and Charlie

Contents

Introduction   xiii

Friendship

CHAPTER 1   *Whatever Gets You in the Game*   3

CHAPTER 2   *Not Everyone Is Going to Like You*   16

CHAPTER 3   *Not Everyone Is Going to Like Me*   26

CHAPTER 4   *The Person Who Hires You Is Your Number One Stockholder*   31

CHAPTER 5   *The Best Gift You Can Give a Stranger Is an Audience*   40

CHAPTER 6   *Up Beats Down*   49

CHAPTER 7   *Ask!*   59

CHAPTER 8   *Don't Call Just When You Need Something*   67

CHAPTER 9   *People Don't Mind Being Used; They Mind Being Discarded*   73

Rivalry

CHAPTER 10   *Grin When You Fight*   79
CHAPTER 11   *It's Not Crowded at the Top*   88
CHAPTER 12   *No One's Ever Late for an Execution*   96
CHAPTER 13   *Nobody Wants a Level Playing Field*   103
CHAPTER 14   *Fire When Ready*   112
CHAPTER 15   *Attack from a Defensive Position*   119

Reputation

CHAPTER 16   *Don't Pick on Someone Your Own Size*   129
CHAPTER 17   *Rites of Passage*   137
CHAPTER 18   *Keep Good Company*   145
CHAPTER 19   *Lowball It!*   150
CHAPTER 20   *When in Doubt, Put It Out*   155
CHAPTER 21   *You Only Get One Reputation*   160

Success

CHAPTER 22   *Aim High*   171
CHAPTER 23   *Speak Up!*   176
CHAPTER 24   *The Bug*   181
CHAPTER 25   *Wherever You Go, That's Where You're Going to Be*   187

Acknowledgments   191
Index   195

My popularity, my happiness and sense of worth
depend to no small extent upon my skill
in dealing with people.

—DALE CARNEGIE

Few things are more shocking to those
who practice the arts of success than
the frank description of those arts.

—LOGAN PEARSALL SMITH

Although every one cannot be
a Gargantua-Napoleon-Bismarck
and walk off with the great bells of Notre Dame,
every one must bear his own universe,
and most persons are moderately interested in learning
how their neighbors have managed to carry theirs.

—The Education of Henry Adams

Introduction

We live in perilous times. This is a handbook for getting ahead in them. It's got all the know-how I've collected on *Hardball* from those successful people I've spent my life studying.

Case in point: President Barack Obama. He didn't elect himself president. He got to the White House by excelling at the two great challenges of life. One, he persuaded people, millions in his case, to do what he wanted them to do. Two, he got past others—rivals, critics, naysayers—who stood in his path.

The premise of this book is straightforward: To get ahead in life you can learn a lot from those who get ahead for a living. Some of what I am going to tell you in this book is counterintuitive, and some is so obvious you'll feel like an idiot for not knowing already. Five nights a week I get to talk with the big shots of our society—the presidential candidates, the chieftains of business, the icons of popular culture. While I try to squeeze the truth out of all of them, the people who make the biggest impression on me and who've really taught me the tricks of getting ahead in life are the politicians. I know that goes against the grain, but so does the shrewdest advice I've grabbed from these guys.

This book is about success. It's everything I've learned about life in four decades of dealing up close and personal with the country's best politicians.

You can say what you want about these masters of power. They get people to vote for them, give money to their campaigns, trust them with their country. They possess this wondrous ability, I've discovered, to get other people to do just what they want them to do.

How? By knowing things. The best of these politicians have a sure grip on human nature. They leave it to the amateurs to believe how people are supposed to behave. They know the secrets of how people actually *do*.

They are good listeners. They know the deep human need to be paid attention to. "Did you ever try listening?" Bill Clinton told a fellow Rhodes scholar when asked his trick for getting the girls. It's the same advice he would give his wife. That "listening tour" of upstate New York made Hillary a United States senator.

Politicians are shameless when asking for things. Being Machiavellian, they know that the more a person gives to them, the more likely that person is to *keep on giving*.

They're upbeat. Barack Obama wasn't the first president to prove the power of optimism. Before Obama gave us "the audacity of hope," Ronald Reagan gave us "morning in America." Before him, John F. Kennedy offered people "high hopes." Before him, Franklin Roosevelt led us in "Happy Days Are Here Again."

I realize that the notion of learning anything of value from politicians cuts against the grain. But what these people can teach us about human nature is priceless: how to get a perfect stranger to like you, help you, root for your success; how to deal with rivals who want the same prize you're chasing; how to build a name for yourself; how to *matter*; and, for those who want to, how to *lead*.

This is not a book of political science. I wouldn't trust one that was. The ability to get along with people, life has taught me, is an *art*. Getting people to do what you want them to, I have further learned, is a *fine* art.

My business is watching and questioning politicians. I can't tell you how instructive their behavior is. You've seen me on *Hardball* in the past twelve years questioning senators, governors, and congressmen. What you haven't seen is the four decades I've devoted to watching and listening to them when they *don't* think I'm doing it. For as long as I've been around them, I've been collecting stories from politicians, quietly distilling from them the traits that separate the professional from the amateur. It has equipped me with valuable lessons about life.

Political traits are in essence the ability to deal with *people*. I'm talking about basic likability, the readiness to listen, to project optimism, to ask for help, to display good cheer in the face of opposition. To learn the traits of the best practitioners is to acquire a treasure chest of ways to persuade and influence people.

So much of life is persuasion, getting people to do what we want them to. We want a child to play by the rules, a boss to appreciate us, our colleagues to see our point of view. We want the person we love to love us back. We prefer friends but we end up facing rivals. We have dreams and we want help in realizing them.

Think of John F. Kennedy or Barack Obama, Ronald Reagan or his old rival Speaker Tip O'Neill, Nancy Pelosi or Hillary Clinton. To them, making new friends, dealing with opponents, getting out their message, and upholding their credibility comes with the territory. It's called *campaigning*.

I realize my enthusiasm for what we can learn from politicians may shock people who are used to my grilling these gentlemen and ladies Monday through Friday on *Hardball* and my dissecting them over the weekend on *The Chris Matthews Show*. The truth is, my TV guests may or may not have a ready answer to my questions about their partisan behavior. They may or may not be up to snuff on a policy question. But when it comes to pushing their own careers, I can assure you, the best politicians know exactly what they're doing.

As I said, they see and exploit the way human beings really behave, not the way we're supposed to. They understand that we much prefer to be listened to than to be talked at, that while we may not mind being used, we resent deeply being made to feel discarded. Politicians also know that no one, whatever lip service he or she may pay to the proposition, wants a level playing field. Gaining an edge is something everyone tries to do. The politician's advantage is his ability to grasp and exploit such basic truths of human nature.

Do you want a campaign that will take you where you want to go in life?

Do you want to find strong friends who will swing doors open for you?

Do you want to recruit allies who will invest their time, trust, and money in you, and back you when the chips are down?

Do you want to make sure your ideas matter?

Do you want to become a leader?

The Hardball Handbook takes a look at the methods of the masters. It shares with you their secrets of success. In the following pages I'll tell you things about them they would never tell me or you: *how they do what they do.*

So, welcome to a noisy, inside peek at people with power and the good you can learn from them. The one thing missing from the memoirs of the great politicians, I have noticed, is the means and methods of their ascent. This book is filled with nothing but.

CHAPTER I

Whatever Gets You in the Game

If you knock long enough and loud enough at the gate
you are bound to wake up somebody.
—HENRY WADSWORTH LONGFELLOW

You cannot win if you're not at the table.
You have to be where the action is.
—BEN STEIN

IT WAS THE THIRD NIGHT of the 2004 Republican National Convention in New York. I was anchoring MSNBC, *Hardball*-style, from a vantage point on Herald Square, a few blocks from Madison Square Garden. The uptown traffic was honking past on the left, the downtown drivers squeezing through on my right. In front of Macy's, protesters were shouting their hatred of President Bush.

Just moments before, an angry Georgia Democrat, Senator Zell Miller, had taken the extraordinary step of addressing the GOP convention. He had delivered a contemptuous attack on his own party's presidential nominee, John Kerry, in which he accused the Massachusetts senator of being weak on national defense. According to Miller, the Democratic candidate would fight the war on terrorism with "spitballs." From my anchor desk on Broadway, I had Miller on a remote hookup from the convention floor. By the expression on the face of the man looming on the giant TV screen before me, I could tell that here was a guy in no mood to answer tough questions.

"Get out of my face!" he told me threateningly. "If you're going to ask a question, step back and let me answer. I wish we lived in the day where you could challenge a man to a duel."

Wow. Had I heard him right? How did I ever land such a job? How had someone like me, hooked on politics since I was a kid, found himself in the very crosshairs of American electoral warfare—to the point where some crazed U.S. senator was proposing a duel? On national television, no less?

Well, as the man said, just step back and let me answer.

The fantasy explanation for how I began hosting *Hardball* five nights a week on MSNBC and *The Chris Matthews Show* on weekends is that someone heard what my dream job was and magically bestowed it upon me. The second— and better—answer is that more than a third of a century ago I managed to get in the game and then worked it from there.

When I came to Washington in 1971, after two years spent overseas, it was like arriving at a party where all the other guests knew one another and no one knew me. The Senate and House offices of Capitol Hill were bustling and cozy—for those with jobs, that is. Everyone but me had a place to go in the morning, a snug workplace to leave at nightfall. I was on the outside looking in.

This is not to say I arrived in the nation's capital feeling uninvited. Ever since the great Kennedy-Nixon fight of 1960 I had felt the allure of politics. The battle over who should run the country was what I had thought about, talked about—and, yes, argued about—since I was in grade school.

My defining goal that sunny Washington winter of my return to America was to become a part of that political world to which I was so deeply drawn. While still a Peace Corps volunteer in Swaziland, where I served from 1968 to the end of 1970, I had gotten a letter from a college friend telling me about his job as legislative assistant to a U.S. senator. The "LA," I knew, was the staffer who helped his boss with the big-picture stuff: writing speeches, drafting legislation, *thinking*. It was the post that the great speechwriter Theodore Sorensen had held in the young John F. Kennedy's Senate office. Transfixed, I had read Sorensen's book *Kennedy* a few months earlier on the overnight train from Mozambique to Rhodesia.

When I arrived in Washington, my strategy for turning myself into a Capitol Hill LA was primitive but direct. I would go door-to-door on the Hill *asking* for such a job. I would start with the congressmen who were Irish Catholic Democrats from the Northeast. I figured that these would be the fellows most likely to hire a gung ho innocent who had gone to Holy Cross, a Jesuit college, and had just gotten home from two years in Africa with Jack Kennedy's Peace Corps.

Though I didn't see it that way at the time, this effort was the first heat in what would be a lifelong race. The goal was getting a job in one of those hallowed Senate or congressional offices. That would be my gate into the world of politics—and a base from which to start my life. I had less than two hundred dollars in my wallet, what was left of my Peace Corps "readjustment allowance" after a slow retreat home through Kenya, Israel, Egypt, and England.

The problem was that if I didn't get a job on the Hill, I had no fallback plan. Though I didn't consciously understand it at the time, the truth was that defeat in this campaign of mine was *not* an option. Lifewise, I had no other ambitions.

My routine was to go up to the Hill each morning and simply trudge from office to office, seeking that prize job of legislative assistant. My tactic—if I dare elevate it to that level—was to walk in bright-eyed and eager and start chatting up the congressman's receptionist. My goal was to secure a meeting with the all-powerful "AA," or administrative assistant, as Senate and House chiefs of staff were called then. That was the person with hire-and-fire authority.

Now, if you're wondering what gave me the nerve to stroll into the offices of strangers like that, consider that I'd spent the previous two years riding my Suzuki 120 into Swazi villages and advising local storeowners in Zulu how to get on with their businesses. Stage fright, I'd learned of necessity, is something you can beat.

Yet as I went knocking on two hundred Senate and House doors, I was straight-armed again and again with every job-searcher's catch-22. You know how it goes: You can't get a job without experience; you can't get experience without first getting a job.

Then one day it happened, just as I'd imagined and

hoped it would. I walked into the office of a Democrat from New Jersey, a high-ranking member of the House Foreign Affairs Committee. As I began my ritual approach to the receptionist, I turned and found myself greeted by a debonair, silver-haired gentleman who introduced himself as the congressman.

When I told him I was just back from the Peace Corps and looking for a job, he invited me into an adjoining room, where he pointed to a plaque on the wall displaying one of the pens that President Lyndon Johnson had used to sign the Peace Corps authorization bill. There was even a note on the plaque from LBJ expressing gratitude to the man now standing next to me for his help on the legislation.

I was overwhelmed by the congressman's attention. Although he resembled nothing so much as a better-dressed, better-groomed version of one of my dad's Knights of Columbus pals, he was in fact a real live United States representative—and there he was selling *me* on a job.

"You don't want to work on the Foreign Affairs Committee," he told me seriously. "You should be working in my office as a legislative assistant." Stunned, I walked away from his office thinking I'd gotten everything I wanted. My planning had been perfect: Irish Catholic . . . Democrat . . . member of the Foreign Affairs Committee. At twenty-five, I was on the verge of being another Ted Sorensen.

So I waited several days to hear back. No word. I then began calling every morning to find out what was happening. I was never put through to the congressman. Finally his Nurse Ratched–like AA got on the phone and delivered the message in a cold voice: "The congressman said to tell you that he couldn't work it out."

Failure.

I would discover only later that the distinguished gentleman from New Jersey had problems on his hands far bigger than the need to fill a legislative assistant's slot. Two
years earlier, while I'd been out of the country, *Life* magazine, then still in its heyday, had run a two-part exposé
headlined "The Congressman and the Hoodlum: The Case
of a Respected Lawmaker Caught Up in the Grasp of Cosa
Nostra." An eight-month investigation had unveiled what
the magazine called the congressman's "second life."

After klieg-lighting his jaunty charm, his commenda-
tions for heroism in World War II and Korea, and his place
on Lyndon Johnson's 1964 short list for running mate, it
got to the dirty backstory:

"Behind the façade of prestige and respectability lives a
man who time and time again has served as a tool and col-
laborator of a Cosa Nostra gang lord." *Life* detailed the
congressman's tape-recorded phone conversations with the
Democratic boss of Bayonne, New Jersey, as he interceded
on behalf of a mob capo to stop the police from probing
local gambling operations.

Then came the story's sugarplum—an unsavory tale of
the time in 1962 when the congressman had summoned a
mob hit man to his house to remove the body of a local
loan shark from the basement.

I learned all of this later, including the embattled congressman's defense, that he was the victim of FBI anger
over his support of federal legislation to restrict "invasions
of privacy."

So the congressman's world was closing in on him in
those early months of 1971. Chased by the law, he was also

getting the bum's rush from his political pals back in Bayonne. He would eventually serve time on federal tax-evasion charges.

Call me a romantic, but I've always chosen to believe that the congressman didn't "work things out" for that LA job because he could see I was too nice a young man to be involved in all that.

A few days later, I renewed my campaign. This time I won what I'd set out to achieve so many times before—an interview with a real life AA. His name was Wayne Owens, and he would change my life. Wayne ran the office for Senator Frank Moss, a well-known Utah Democrat. He had worked as Robert F. Kennedy's western states coordinator during RFK's ultimately tragic presidential campaign, and later as a top aide to Senator Ted Kennedy. I would soon learn that Wayne was planning his own race for Congress in his native state of Utah.

Most important to me, he loved the fact that I'd been in the Peace Corps. Also, it struck me later, he liked that I was a Catholic who'd gone to college in Massachusetts, that is, in Kennedy country. A devout Mormon from the West, he made it clear at our first meeting that he valued the assets I brought to the table. They may well have been the reason I got in to see him in the first place.

After that meeting with Wayne, the prospect of my becoming a U.S. senator's legislative assistant suddenly looked a lot brighter. But first, as a test of my abilities, he asked me to draft an answer to a complicated letter that a prominent Salt Lake City constituent had sent Senator Moss on a tax matter.

When I returned with it several days later—having

leaned on staffers I'd gotten to know at my hometown Philadelphia congressman's office, along with an IRS technical expert to whom they referred me—I was able to deliver exactly what Wayne was looking for.

Then came the bad news. Wayne *wanted* to hire me, but the only job he had available, even after my passing that grueling take-home exam, was the position of Capitol policeman. The idea was that I would toil in Moss's office three or four hours a day answering complicated mail and writing short speeches for the boss to read on the Senate floor, then go to work from three to eleven P.M. as a cop guarding the Capitol.

It was one of those patronage gigs that senators and congressmen had to offer, like working in the mailroom or operating the House elevator. They were start-from-the-bottom slots, usually awarded to well-connected sons or daughters attending Georgetown or George Washington.

In my case, I was being given a chance to say yes, grab the salary, put in my time—and wait to see what came next.

"It'll pay for the groceries," Wayne pointed out, seeing the disappointed expression on my face.

Glumly, I agreed. I had a college degree, a year behind me spent working on a doctorate in economics, two years of challenging service in Africa, and eighty dollars left in my pocket.

With a few hours of training on the House of Representatives firing range, I was soon walking around the Capitol with a .38 Special in my holster. One night I sat armed and ready outside a door containing the "Pentagon Papers," though they'd already been published by *The Washington Post* and *The New York Times*.

Usually I manned a lonely post somewhere deep in the Capitol basement, studying the *Congressional Record,* writing and rewriting speeches for Senator Moss. I met the other patronage cops, who were paying for law school as they moonlighted in what one called a "Mack Sennett costume." But I also got to know the country boys, those former MPs who made long daily commutes from as far as West Virginia, and who guarded the U.S. Capitol with dedication.

"You know why the little man loves his country," Sergeant Leroy Taylor once explained to me. "It's because it's all he's got." And I remember the middle-aged guy who stopped me on the West Front one sunny day before a big antiwar demonstration to say, "Hit one of them for me, will you?" Yeah, I remember that fellow. For someone who just spent two years in Africa with the Peace Corps, it was an abrupt but useful reunion with a country divided over Vietnam.

As I said, most of my time was spent reading and practicing speechwriting in an underground Capitol tunnel. When nightfall came and the tourists, the congressmen, and their staffers left, I was pretty much by myself down there. It was, in fact, the safest place in the neighborhood. The only danger I faced while on duty came during those evening jaunts across Pennsylvania Avenue to grab a quick supper at one of the old-style eateries that used to line the street.

What if an actual robbery had been under way in this then-high-crime neighborhood? What if someone—a bystander or the robber—had taken me for a real cop? It was a terrible possibility that luckily never happened.

In the end, I developed a strange liking for the job.

Every day at three P.M. I'd put on that starched police shirt, tie, trousers, and .38 and feel that a whole other life was kicking in. On top of that, the history really got to me. I remember one night lingering alone in the Capitol Rotunda, where John F. Kennedy had lain in state those cold November hours in 1963; I was lost in reverie as I conjured up those memories.

But I also dearly wanted things to change. I was arriving at Senator Moss's office each morning and leaving the Capitol twelve hours later, day after day. By the time summer came, I went to Wayne and said I was tired of waiting for that legislative assistant job I'd come looking for in the first place.

To my surprise and pleasure, he looked at me and said okay. Such ready agreement offered me another lesson I would absorb along the way: *If you want something, ask for it!*

And so in September 1971, I was finally out there on the floor of the United States Senate, a legislative assistant hard at work on issues of government, minimum wage, and the federal budget. I was writing speeches, suggesting amendments to bills, even drafting an important measure on post-Vietnam-era economic readjustment. I was absorbed in my new job and loving it.

The "cop" part of my résumé continues to startle some people. To others, my Irish American roots give it a certain poetry. And those months of guarding the U.S. Capitol with that .38 Police Special might even illustrate a bit of wisdom attributed to the gangster Al Capone, though it's not the way it was meant: "You get more with a kind word and a *gun* than with just a kind word."

But the gun was now in my past and I was on my way. I had emerged from my basement lair into the thrilling arena of American politics. There had been a small door and I had squeezed through it.

When people ask me how I "got where I got" and how I have the nerve to put leaders, officials, and dignitaries on the hot seat, my answer begins with my experience working for politicians. Yet it was a training ground from which I might never have benefited had I not accepted and carried out that first less-than-ideal assignment.

Experience counts. That phrase may not have sold the American public on Richard Nixon back in 1960 when he ran against John F. Kennedy for president. But it has worked for me. Now every time I watch a U.S. senator hold forth on C-SPAN, my mind zips back to those months when I was in my mid-twenties and at home on the Senate floor myself, assisting on amendments, listening as the distinguished gentleman from Utah read words I'd composed.

Eventually, to my great joy, I'd find myself in that ultimate Ted Sorensen job, writing speeches for a president. This means that whenever I watch any president give a speech, I recall those heady days in my early thirties when I sat at my Selectric II on Air Force One, grappling for the words and phrases that would best serve my boss, Jimmy Carter, on his next stop.

That was the late 1970s. Now jump forward to the 1980s, when for a half dozen years I began each day at the side of a legendary Speaker of the House as he stood his ground against "the Great Communicator," Ronald Reagan. It was an amazing ringside seat, and it surely informs the way I see Nancy Pelosi, the first woman Speaker, lead-ing her troops.

And whenever I hear about a campaign anywhere, I flash back to all those races I lived firsthand, with their winners' thrilling sense of destiny and the tears on the faces of the losers.

How did I wind up with such a grand political educa-tion? After all, there are no written qualifications for all the jobs I had before I got into journalism twenty years ago. There were no civil service tests, no formal vetting process for those slots working for senators, presidents, and con-gressmen. It was all opportunity *and* politics.

I had had a plan but remained flexible, seizing opportu-nities along the way. I asked for what I wanted and, on key occasions, somebody said yes. At each stage I took what-ever door was open.

I wanted to be there and carried out a campaign that got me there.

That's the heart of it, I've learned. Nobody out there is curious about the profound ideas bouncing around in your brain. Nobody is checking in with you to see what ambi-tions they might be able to help you realize. Nobody cares what dreams are yours as you lay your head on the pillow each night.

It's all up to you. If you want to push your ideas, ambi-tions, or dreams, you have to get out there and champion them. You need to be able to face rejection, hostility, and, more often, indifference. The higher your ambitions take you, the more stamina you'll need, the more willingness to get a "No!" slammed in your face. The more failure you can accept, the greater your chance of success.

Yes, I was hooked on politics long before I began my career in and around it, but it took more than that fascination. What I had to do was hit the bricks and make it all come true.

You can't tell which road is going to take you where you want to go. Not at first. You may have to try them all. But never, ever look down on the job that starts you off in the business you have chosen. Being a Capitol police officer hadn't been in my original game plan, but it took me through the door. As it turned out, I enjoyed it and wound up proud of that stint, not just because of where that job led me but for what it taught me as well.

Bottom Line

Whatever your ambition, you can't win unless you're in the game. If you want to be a lawyer, go to any law school you can get into. Same with medicine. If you want to make movies, find a way to break in. The people who show up get the chances. Get it? To win the contest, you first have to be a contestant.

CHAPTER 2

Not Everyone Is Going to Like You

Always forgive your enemies—
but never forget their names.
—Robert F. Kennedy

The people have spoken—the bastards!
—Dick Tuck

Bill Clinton may be the best politician I've ever seen. He was elected governor of Arkansas six times, president of the United States twice. He managed to survive a zealous partisan drive, albeit one triggered by his own misconduct, to remove him from office. Clinton rose to his high-wire political exploits—even critics would admit—having started from the bottom. His father, Bill Blythe, a traveling salesman, had three wives prior to Clinton's mother, and several children, not all of them through marriage. Three months before Clinton was born, Blythe was killed in a road accident.

Clinton's stepfather, who helped raise him and whose surname he later took, was a drunk and a wife-beater. At fourteen, the future president would confront his stepdad,

Roger Clinton, and warn him not to hit his mother again. The man never did. This hard-knocks childhood definitely helped prepare Bill Clinton for the surges of lethal hostility he would face later.

In my living room, I have a picture of him greeting my son, Michael, who was nine at the time. It was the Saturday before the 1992 New Hampshire primary, and Clinton was going door-to-door handing out videocassettes about himself. His campaign had put out the word that such political retailing was the only way that their candidate, burdened by charges of draft evasion, was going to get his message past the media and directly to voters.

Whatever you think of Clinton, this New Hampshire exercise was a public display of the man's inner toughness, not to mention a dazzling bit of campaign showmanship. ABC had just gone on the air exhibiting a Vietnam-era letter that young Bill Clinton had sent to the head of the Reserve Officers Training Corps at the University of Arkansas, thanking the army colonel for "saving" him from the draft.

It was the smoking gun of Clinton's youthful gambit to avoid wartime military service by convincing both his local draft board and the ROTC that he was committed to taking officer's training, a promise he hoped never to have to keep. But the wily Governor Clinton wasn't going to let the unassailable fact of such a document stand in his way.

Rather than spend the last weekend before the New Hampshire primary fielding questions about his notorious "draft letter," he invited journalists—like me—to follow him with our cameras and notepads as he went down the street talking to real voters. He used the press to take on the press.

I have often thought back on the resolve displayed by Bill Clinton in those weeks. He'd already cut his losses after a lounge singer named Gennifer Flowers called a New York press conference to claim a thirteen-year affair with him. Despite the unmistakable sound of his voice in a recorded phone conversation with Flowers, his people had curtly dismissed the tape as edited. He was now under fire for the draft letter, a far more damaging episode and one that cut to the heart of a presidential run by the first candidate who had been a college student in the rebellious 1960s.

Yet here he was walking door-to-door with those videotapes explaining to voters what Bill Clinton intended to do for them.

With his rivals rooting for his campaign to collapse, with the media gleefully reporting the worst, this guy was the Energizer Bunny, the one who just keeps on beating his drum.

Take this lesson from a great politician: *Not everyone is going to like you.*

Certainly not everyone likes Bill Clinton. When he was a student at Georgetown University, he was elected class president as a freshman and sophomore. Yet when he ran for president of the student body in his junior year, by which time his classmates had presumably gotten to know him better, he was beaten—and badly—by a campus nerd. He had gotten a reputation for being "too slick."

Clinton faced the same problem when he entered grown-up politics. When he made his maiden run for public office, a 1974 congressional race, he lost. No problem: Most people lose on their first outing. Yet after convincing the voters of Arkansas to elect him governor in 1978, he had the unpleasant experience of seeing them dump him from the job the next time around.

But if there was something about Clinton the voters didn't like, he refused to let it kill his ambition. He ran for governor five more times and never got beat again.

And so in 1992, right before our eyes in the Granite State, he was offering himself to the voters, complete with all his flaws. His earlier lead in the polls had vaporized, but Clinton stood alone in one college gym after another, with hundreds gathered around him each time. He answered every question asked.

Hard-bitten journalists sat there in the bleachers awed by his ability to take so many shots and show so little fear. My friend Rick Hertzberg, then at *The New Republic*, confessed after one such Clinton performance that he could imagine many things that others of his and Clinton's age could do, but not this. How, he marveled, could anyone of our generation be so confident, so commanding, under such public assault?

That Tuesday, Clinton's strength of will was in full evidence. There he was, on the night of the 1992 New Hampshire Democratic primary, striding before the national TV cameras to crown himself "the Comeback Kid." When I saw him the next morning on the set of *Good Morning America* surrounded by a phalanx of blue suits, he was every inch the winner. No one seemed to have noticed that Clinton had, in fact, just *lost* the primary election—which earlier polls had shown him winning—by eight percentage points to the tragically ill former senator from Massachusetts, Paul Tsongas.

Clinton's relentless salesmanship had so dazzled the media and the public, he had so capitalized on his diminished prospects, that even a weak second place could be spun into a "comeback," a triumph.

Clinton's packaging of that New Hampshire victory, following as it did his defiant head-down campaigning the weekend before, was not a onetime thing. Rather, it was a test for which he'd spent his life practicing. It was this same extraordinary ability to stand tall in the face of mass hostility that he would rely on again and again.

The coup Clinton pulled off in New Hampshire in 1992 was but a precursor of his feat in 1998: an entire year spent surviving the fallout from the revelation of his sexual dalliance with White House staffer Monica Lewinsky and his subsequent lying under oath about the affair.

Staffers and friends close to him during the first days after the story broke could not believe how he kept his focus on the job so razor sharp. The media—me included!—were out there shouting for the truth, and his Republican opponents were hollering for his head. Yet even after being impeached by the House of Representatives, as he was that autumn, he showed up for work and rarely let us see him sweat.

In June 2006 I witnessed a rare moment when Clinton came clean on just what it takes, on how he manages to achieve that inner command he's repeatedly exhibited. He was speaking off the cuff to a room filled with Rhodes scholars and other high-achieving, ambitious young people. "You cannot let what people say define who you are," he told the rapt group. "You have to have an inner core where people can't get to you."

Clinton survived because he trained himself early to take a punch. "You know who I am," he once dared Speaker Newt Gingrich, his adversary in the 1995 government shutdown. "I'm the big rubber clown doll you had as a kid, and every time you hit it, it bounces back. That's me!"

From the moment Bill Clinton weathered that defeat for president of the student body at Georgetown, he had come to terms with how the world worked. There were those who liked him and would be loyal to him for life. There were those who thought him a hopeless phony and tried to ignore him, and there were those who envied and resented his political success and would try to destroy him.

To this day, Clinton has succeeded by embracing those who like him, accepting opposition as part of life's contest. He ran for Congress that first time by emptying a large cardboard box of matchbooks and bar napkins bearing the scribbled names of people with whom he'd once clicked. That box was his campaign war chest. Ever since, he's been defeating and dismaying those whose names would never appear on a Clinton bar napkin.

Politicians have no problem with being both liked and disliked. They take it in stride. Like Hyman Roth, the old mobster in *Godfather II*, they know what they've gotten into. It's the business they have chosen. A Zogby poll taken in March 2007 found that not just Barack Obama and Hillary Clinton but each of the well-known candidates had at least three of ten voters saying they'd never cast a ballot for them.

Why? Because opposition is built into any democratic system. Each candidate faces automatic antipathy from some sizable group. Politicians learn to live with this. They awake each day fully aware that a lot of onlookers would just love to witness their professional demise.

In this sense, politicians teach us how to *take* it.

If everybody liked you, you'd have few worries in this world, no real challenges. Doors would fly open for you. All your ideas would be admiringly received, your ambitions instantly satisfied, your dreams and fantasies fulfilled.

But that's not the way the world works. Some potential allies, if you're reasonably fortunate, will like you immediately. Then there will be others you will be able to win over with some effort. Finally, there are those you'll never be able to enlist to your team.

The whole trick of life is therefore to (a) find people who like you on first meeting, (b) put effort into winning over those people you can, and (c) recognize those whom, to use Donald Trump's phrase, you need to "work around."

Again, this is what politicians call *campaigning*. It's something you'll find you have to do in life even if you never run in a single election.

In *Hardball*, my first book, I told the story of the Texas congressman who, during the course of my 1971 job-seeking odyssey through the halls of the U.S. Capitol, rejected me at our first meeting.

"I would say that people in my district, and I don't mean any offense by this, would be put off by your way of speaking and your hair style," he told me bluntly. I reasonably assumed that in this Texan's county, the first was too fast, the second too long. Then, going in for the kill, he explained that the folks back home would look at me and figure I'd brought home some "idealistic notions" from Africa with me.

Having dropped a bomb on my prospects of ever getting hired by the likes of him, the Texas representative offered up by way of consolation some useful advice. "Politics is like selling insurance door-to-door, which is what I used to do before getting into this business. Some people will go for you and some won't. You knock on a hundred doors; you get nine people to invite you back for a sales pitch. Of the nine, three will buy the policy. You have to sell three people to do all right, but you'll never find those three unless you knock on the hundred doors to start with."

I've carried that hard-knocks wisdom with me ever since. He was telling me that some folks go for you—and some don't. To get ahead, you have to keep putting up with the nos to get to the yeses—which is what he encouraged me to do.

Tip O'Neill, whose AA I became in 1981, was an old political pro who made himself into a Democratic standard bearer by taking on "the Great Communicator," Ronald Reagan, at a time when nobody else would. I was there by his side the entire way. It was the best, certainly the toughest, political job I ever had.

I spent thousands of hours with this legend of a politician. On the calmer days, when we'd sit there in the back room of his Capitol office, he'd share old war stories. I remember his recalling with amazement how Jack Kennedy, who had held O'Neill's congressional seat before him, could never stop fretting about some guy back in Cambridge or Boston who didn't like him.

O'Neill, who had been in the rough-and-tumble of Massachusetts politics ever since he'd graduated from Boston College in the 1930s, realized long ago that not being liked came with the territory.

As Ronald Reagan's most prominent rival, he boarded airplanes always aware that more than half the passengers, especially those in first class, took pleasure in voting against man-of-the-people liberal Democrats like him. What really got to the church-going O'Neill was when the Roman Catholic nuns he met told him to be "nicer to President Reagan."

Over the years I've sized up politicians' faults and strengths. Watching Tip O'Neill at close range, I saw how those who intend to accomplish something have to take the brickbats. He got up each morning and brushed his teeth, shined his shoes, dressed, and went to work, knowing how many fellow citizens wanted him to get out of the way of the Reagan Revolution. Throughout the long years of 1981 and 1982, he was a man vilified simply for doing his job as leader of the national political opposition.

Yet if he hadn't stood tough for what he believed in— the needs of the old, the sick, and the poor—he wouldn't have become the folk hero he did.

What the savvy veterans like Tip O'Neill always knew intuitively, the amateurs and rookies are forced to find out. In the business of Washington, D.C., politics, the fuel is ambition and alliances; the engine is rivalry; and the output is deals, reputations, presidencies.

In this world, facing opposition is as inevitable as Monday morning. Wherever there are limited numbers of prizes, wherever the supply of fame and prestige is rationed, envy and fear are natural by-products. Never, ever forget that there are those whose place in the system depends on *not* rooting for you.

Bottom Line

Not everyone is going to like you in this world. There are several good reasons for that. One is that you and your opponent want the same prize. The best attitude to take is that rivalry is as normal as friendship. Learn to live with the first; build your life on the second.

CHAPTER 3

Not Everyone Is Going to Like Me

*I've learned that people only really pay attention
to what they discover for themselves.*
—from the film PRETTY POISON

*Pay attention to your enemies,
for they are the first to discover your mistakes.*
—ANTISTHENES

THE PROGRESS OF A CAREER often looks smoother from the outside. I long ago became adept at displaying my personal list of political jobs I've held like a tight-fitting stack of tuna cans, each solidly supporting the one above it: two years as a U.S. senator's legislative assistant, three years on the Senate Budget Committee, four years at the White House, the last two as a presidential speechwriter, six years as a top aide to a legendary Speaker of the House. After that would come a decade and a half with newspapers, first as Washington bureau chief and nationally syndicated columnist for the *San Francisco Examiner*, then as national columnist for the *San Francisco Chronicle*, followed by a solid stretch of television with *Hardball* and *The Chris Matthews Show*.

Some people, not necessarily fans, regard everything I've accomplished as outrageous good luck. The reality is far less glossy. There have been some rocky times along the way that you don't see in the résumé.

It took ten years to get from my patronage job as a Capitol policeman to my position as AA to Tip O'Neill, arguably the highest staff post in the U.S. Congress. Please don't think the climb was all onward and upward.

The most trying time—the late fall of 1972 to the late summer of 1974—coincided with that dramatic era in our country's political history, from Richard Nixon's landslide reelection to his rough dethroning in August 1974.

I began 1972 happy in my role as a Senate legislative assistant, drafting amendments, writing speeches, sometimes sitting alongside my boss, Senator Moss, right there on the Senate floor. I was twenty-six years old and had an underground parking space where every day I was delighted to put the secondhand Mercedes-Benz I'd bought from an Egyptian official at the World Bank. I was riding high.

Then the trouble came. It started when Wayne Owens, who'd brought me aboard and won me the upgrade to legislative assistant, quit his job as Senator Moss's top aide and returned to Utah to run for Congress. His successor as the senator's AA was a quiet political rival of Wayne's, a fellow who harbored electoral plans of his own one day.

Faced with this new order, I made a number of mistakes that would lead, at least temporarily, to a diminution in the excellent graces in which Senator Moss held me.

The first mistake came from following my heart, not my head. In September 1972, the senator sent me out to

Utah to perform some pre-election scut work for the local Democratic Party, a task that involved updating voter rolls. I couldn't keep my mind on the project. I couldn't resist getting pulled mind and heart into Owens's daring challenge to an incumbent Republican. To avoid any ethical conflict I called Senator Moss back in Washington and asked that he "take me off the payroll."

By meticulously averting any trouble, I thought I was being loyal, protecting *him* from any charge of impropriety. Looking back, it's now obvious that my actions could have struck the senator—who'd given me every opportunity, including a recent raise—as a clear breach of loyalty.

The second mistake at that juncture was not showing the proper enthusiasm for the new AA's own political ambitions. At the very least, I could have been less critical when he took me to lunch one day and asked me what I thought of his running a campaign by raising large amounts of money and spending it on TV advertising, a gambit that would become common in later years. Displaying my outright skepticism wasn't very politic of me.

I had made the classic error of dividing and confusing my loyalties. The retaliation would be swift.

The telephone call came early the morning after Election Day 1972, *way* too early given the festivities of the night before. It was from the new AA. He said I was wanted at the office "now."

The day before, Democratic candidate George McGovern had been utterly wiped out by Richard Nixon. However, the good news was that out in Utah, Wayne Owens had bucked the big Republican tide to defeat the incumbent. Now I was to get a political verdict of my own.

When I showed up at Senator Moss's office, my un-suspected nemesis, the AA, told me he assumed I'd be going to work now for Wayne. But even if that wasn't the case, my services were no longer needed in the senator's office.

I never knew what role Senator Moss himself had in what amounted to my firing. What I do know is that he continued to support me. Even that unhappy morning, he suggested, when I finally got in to see him, that I might make a run for public office in my own right one day. "Maybe you ought to dip a little deeper into these political waters," he said.

Senator Moss would, in fact, remain a strong booster. In 1974, following another switch in AAs, I was brought back to write speeches. Moss then pushed hard and person-ally for a prestigious position for me on the newly created Senate Committee on the Budget. "You want a good man?" one of the office secretaries later said, reciting by heart Moss's sales pitch to Senate colleague Edmund Muskie of Maine, who'd been named chairman of the committee, "*He*'s a good man!"

Hearing what he had said on my behalf came as a real confidence-builder, because it had hurt losing that first much-prized job as a senator's LA. Not only had it been hu-miliating, but it made me see that what had seemed like a firm rung on the ladder to success in Washington was, in fact, more precarious than I'd realized. But forfeiting that first political job in late 1972 got me off my butt. Just as coming to Washington without connections had necessi-tated my campaign for that LA job, being thrown out of work forced me to climb new mountains.

Someone had turned on me, and I had to take the consequences.

Nine years later, with four years working at the White House, including the job of presidential speechwriter, behind me, Speaker of the House Thomas P. "Tip" O'Neill, Jr., would appoint me *his* AA. Through the next half dozen years of daily partisan and philosophical rivalry with President Ronald Reagan, I would serve in the middle of the action.

Bottom Line

It's a hard thing to come up against a person who deliberately intends you harm. The solution is to take note of your adversary and even closer note of what you did to make yourself vulnerable to him. You can't reduce the number of rivals you face in life or even the number of mistakes you make. But you can cut down on the number of mistakes you make *twice*.

CHAPTER 4

The Person Who Hires You Is Your Number One Stockholder

*It is not so much our friends' help that helps us
as the confident knowledge that they will help us.*
—Epicurus

It's not what you know; it's who you know.
—MY MOTHER

WHEN NANCY PELOSI, the first woman to head the U.S. House of Representatives, backed her ally Jack Murtha in a failed run for majority leader in late 2006, critics called it the new Speaker's first mistake.

That's not how a professional would score it.

Politics, like most human relations, is based on give-and-take. You look out for the people who have helped you in the past. Either that, or don't plan on having the chips to cash in in the future.

Jack Murtha came up the way the Pelosi family did, through street-corner politics. A combat veteran of Vietnam, Murtha had run a car wash in Johnstown, Pennsylvania. Pelosi herself is the daughter of a row-house politician in Baltimore. When her dad was elected mayor, he kept a "favors list" of those who helped get him there.

Like Saint Peter, Nancy's father would use this ledger to assign patronage. These were the folks who would land city jobs when they opened up, be handed promotions when the time came.

In November 2006, the Democrats won a majority of House seats, giving Pelosi the speakership and placing Murtha at the top of her favors list. He had been her campaign manager when she'd run several years earlier for majority whip, the post that put her in line for the top job. He had moved mountains for her. Among the people who count—in this case, members of Congress and their extended networks of staffers and other dependents—it didn't hurt brand-new Speaker Nancy Pelosi one bit to be seen looking out for the guy who had helped her get there.

I know this world. In those hours we spent together in the Speaker's private office, Tip O'Neill loved to repeat how the old crowd in North Cambridge, Massachusetts, handed out "snow buttons" to loyalists. Those with the buttons were put on the city payroll when the heavy New England winter snows hit. For those fortunate guys, every snowfall meant cash in their pockets.

"Loyalty is everything in this business," Tip reminded me early one morning back in 1984. The tone of his voice carried an underlying message: *Don't forget it*. The reason for his admonition that A.M. was my having been quoted in *The New York Times* that day being far too evenhanded about Walter Mondale and Gary Hart, the two guys running for the Democratic presidential nomination. Mondale, Tip's candidate, had called him to complain. Tip didn't want me out there *trimming* his guy. I learned later that my boss had never forgiven Hart, who as campaign manager for 1972 Democratic presidential candidate George McGovern had helped dump the regular Massachusetts convention delegates—Tip included—for "the cast of *Hair*." O'Neill held Hart responsible for bringing the Democratic Party down to utter defeat, and had told him so to his face.

Friendship and loyalty are the gold standard of politics *and* life. They certainly are in the U.S. House of Representatives, a body of 435 members that is as much governed by cliques as any high school cafeteria. For a half dozen years that world was *my* world.

As a top assistant to Tip, I would spend Tuesdays through Thursdays strolling back and forth across the corridor from Room 209, where I sat in front of the Speaker's ceremonial office, to the House floor. The desk that went with my job had a lot of tradition attached to it, and, as its current occupant, I was part of the anthropology of the place.

If I got to work early I could smell the heavy morning aroma of bacon and toast wafting up from the Members' Dining Room. You could predict who would be sitting at what tables around the room. Over to the left would be the brooding black Irishmen, Joe Early of Worcester and Eddie Boland of Springfield, the little guy who had been Tip's roommate for twenty years before Tip brought his wife, Millie, down to Washington. Closer to the door would be another predictable duo: Tip's Boston College classmate Bob Griffin, a Chrysler lobbyist, and Tip's trusted senior aide Leo Diehl, who, after a rough redistricting a half century earlier, had sacrificed his seat in the Massachusetts legislature so that his pal Tip O'Neill could keep his.

Another kind of tribal ritual was the Tuesday night dinners attended by a younger crowd: Barbara Boxer, George Miller, and Leon Panetta, from the San Francisco area, and the rest of a regular pack hailing from the Chicago and New York suburbs. All married, with their spouses back home, they'd meet for Italian or Chinese at one or another cheap spot on Capitol Hill. It seemed to me it was a social phalanx to guard against the loneliness—and avoid the temptation—that too often accompanies such jobs.

Look down on the House floor today during a debate and if you're in the know, you'll be able to spot similar gangs. There's the "Gym caucus," the guys who meet in the House gym in late afternoon for pickup basketball games. This daily "heart attack prevention" habit is totally bipartisan and creates curious alliances. Gym buddies John Kasich, a deficit hawk Republican from Ohio, and antiwar Democrat Ron Dellums of California once teamed up to go after a case of Pentagon waste.

Or there's the "Pennsylvania corner," an ancient place of power on the House floor. Located on the far Democratic side of the aisle, it's manned by tough, pro-labor types forever wanting to get home to their districts. "Vote!" you'll hear them yelling late on Thursday evening. "Vote!" And presiding over it all—the sensitive matter of congressional pay, the general scuttlebutt, the leadership strategies—is the insider's insider, Jack Murtha.

This is the clubhouse world from which Nancy Pelosi

made her pick for House majority leader. It's not all that different from the world Tip O'Neill knew coming up, and that, along with him, I knew. Today they play basketball in the gym. In the old days (I can hear Tip's voice, as he loved that phrase) members played cards—gin rummy or poker—on different nights of the week at the University and Army-Navy clubs. "Many a day I've seen that flag at dawn," Tip would confide to me as he gestured to the Stars and Stripes that flies over the Capitol, alluding wistfully to those long-lost all-night card games.

A lot of politics has to do with whom you like to hang around with. When Tip O'Neill was looking to find his new administrative assistant, I heard from his son Kip that his father wanted "someone he feels comfortable with." Being lucky enough to fit that bill, I wound up with the best political job of my life.

Each time I hear that someone has landed a Cabinet or important staff job in Washington, I always try to understand the human mechanics behind it. Soon enough, the answer reveals itself. There's always a backstory, a personal history. Somebody once worked for somebody, or went to school with them, or shared the political trenches in a past administration.

I have my own way of thinking about such moments of recognition.

You know those little metal clickers that kids used to play with around Thanksgiving? They're called "crickets." Allied paratroopers actually used them at Normandy when they jumped behind Nazi lines and needed to team up with one another in the dark. I have this cricket that goes off in my head every time I can track a major Washington appointment to some old friendship. Why? Because it renews my faith in how things work.

It's about repaying loyalty, remembering who helped out along the way. People understand it. They respect it. And it reminds us how valuable it is to make and keep friends in this world.

Dick Cheney was deputy White House chief of staff under President Gerald Ford back in the 1970s. His boss, the chief of staff, was a former congressman from Illinois named Donald Rumsfeld. When Rumsfeld was appointed secretary of defense, Cheney succeeded him as Ford's top staffer. Three decades later, when Cheney secured the position of vice president on the George W. Bush ticket—a nod that would make him the most influential veep in history—he supported his old colleague for a Pentagon comeback.

Every door that swings wide for you has somebody on the other side opening it. The principle to remember here is that once a person has made a bet on you, they're likely to do it again. Hiring someone is a very personal thing. It's buying stock in someone else's success. The key is to think of each person who gives you a job or promotion as a stockholder, someone who has a deep investment in you.

Every job I've ever gotten has come from a relationship that clicked. I had been brought into the White House in 1977 after a single meeting with Richard Pettigrew, a former Speaker of the Florida House of Representatives who was then advisor to President Carter on government reorganization. Then Hendrik Hertzberg, whom I became friends with there, proposed me for an open slot on the Carter speechwriting staff.

It turned out to be the most fun I ever had in politics—staying up late at night, hanging out with the other speechwriters and our girlfriends. My girlfriend, Kathleen Cunningham, and I got married during this magical time. Flying on Air Force One, typing remarks for the president's next stop as the plane shot skyward could only have been better if Carter had won a second term.

I owe my job working for Tip O'Neill initially to Marty Franks, who was research director of the Democratic National Committee. As presidential speechwriters, we relied on Marty throughout the 1980 campaign. Afterward he and Congressman Tony Coelho of California recruited me to the Democratic Congressional Campaign Committee, where Marty was the staff director, to help the Speaker take on President Reagan. Within months I got my battlefield promotion: When the Speaker's AA retired, in mid-1981, the great man pronounced me his successor. "I like the way you carry yourself," he said that thrilling day when he made it official.

I owe my start in full-time journalism six years later to a lunch I had in San Francisco with Larry Kramer, a friend of mine from his days as metro editor of *The Washington Post*. By 1987, Larry had become executive editor of the *San Francisco Examiner*, the *Citizen Kane* flagship of the Hearst empire. After an enjoyable meal he popped the question: Did I want to write a column once a week? *Did* I! It had been my fantasy for years, ever since I began reading James J. Kilpatrick in the *Raleigh News & Observer* as a University of North Carolina grad student. I jumped at the two-hundred-dollar-a-week offer. A few months later, Larry called up from San Francisco to offer me the job of Washington bureau chief, and promoted me to twice-a-week columnist. Within two months, my column was being syndicated nationally. I could hardly believe it.

How did I get on television? I owe that opportunity to Howard Stringer. In the late 1980s, he was president of CBS News and the first person to encourage me to go on the air. When I got the full-time job with the *Examiner* he escorted me down the hall to meet David Corvo, who was then the executive producer of *CBS This Morning*. It wasn't long before Corvo signed me up as a weekly commentator.

The chance to host my own TV show was also rooted in a personal connection.

In the early 1990s, I went to dinner with author Joe McGinniss, who had made his name originally with *The Selling of the President 1968*, the backroom story of how Richard Nixon used TV in 1968 in his second run for the White House. Joe was now a bestselling true-crime writer. A Holy Cross grad like me, he invited me to join him afterward for drinks with Roger Ailes, then best known as the media guru for Nixon, Ronald Reagan, and the elder George Bush.

Roger and I hit it off immediately and kept in contact about the idea of doing a fast-paced TV show capsulizing all the news—political, entertainment, sports—in a tight weekly half hour. (That idea still excites me.) In 1994, Ailes was hired by NBC to run CNBC and a new cable network called America's Talking, the forerunner of MSNBC.

Soon Roger, a man known for acting on his gut instinct,

gave me a two-hour-a-night news and talk show. Since the O. J. Simpson murder trial was just getting under way, we could provide our viewers with a nightly diet of juicy red meat. Before leaving NBC to start Fox News, which was, of course, an enormous success, Roger switched me over to CNBC, where first *Politics* and then *Hardball* were born.

So for me, it all came down to the *personal*. After all the preparation in the world, I've gotten my breaks from individual human beings who decided to give me those breaks.

To grasp further the power of the personal factor, consider the unlikely friendship between Ronald Reagan and Soviet leader Mikhail Gorbachev. Someone once asked Gorbachev how he and Reagan, men of totally different worldviews, managed to sit down and simply end the Cold War. "I liked him," Gorbachev answered. For his part, Reagan told people that he had a surprising chemistry with his Russian counterpart. He compared that rapport to his odd-couple, after-hours camaraderie with Tip O'Neill.

Bottom Line

Loyalty. Friendship. Investment. Reward. Never underestimate these factors. They're the cement of human politics. If you wish to construct a career, build it with what you know. Knowledge, talent, and effort are the building blocks, but personal relations are what hold everything together. As Tip O'Neill said, "Loyalty is everything in this business"—whatever the business.

CHAPTER 5

The Best Gift You Can Give a Stranger Is an Audience

*Many a man would rather you heard his story
than granted his request.*
—Lord Chesterfield

*Listening, not imitation, may be the sincerest form of flattery. . . . If you
want to influence someone, listen to what he says.*
—Dr. Joyce Brothers

WHEN HE WAS a Yank at Oxford, Bill Clinton had a reputation as someone who knew how to get the girls. A fellow Rhodes scholar who was waging a losing battle for the woman of his dreams asked Clinton for advice. "Have you ever thought about *listening*?" the expert from Hope, Arkansas, told him authoritatively.

I wish I had had him as my friend back in those days. I always thought the best way to a girl's heart was to drink beer and brag about myself. Clinton knew and still does that the way to anyone's heart is to listen to it, to let the other person speak.

"To have someone listening to you is flattering," he told his Oxford pal. "If you let them do the talking, they'll be far more interested in you."

As biographer David Maraniss recalls it, Clinton used the same tactic to score good grades. As a college student at Georgetown, Bill was famous for being able to read the professors. He would wow his classmates by predicting just what questions would be on the exams. That's because he listened in class, really *heard* what the professor most cared about. This is something I've been telling my kids: Pay attention to what the teacher personally is trying to teach.

Observers have never stopped marveling at Clinton's skill in this department. Even in the chaos of a campaign, with all hell breaking loose, he could shut out everything but the person he was listening to. It's an extraordinary talent. To be able to truly listen shows respect in ways that all the speeches in the world cannot.

And Bill Clinton has had a star pupil.

In the fall of 1999, a Quinnipiac University poll asked the voters of New York State some questions about the upcoming race to fill the seat of Senator Daniel Patrick Moynihan, who was not seeking reelection. Forty-nine percent said it "bothered" them that a particular candidate was "currently not a resident of New York." Only 40 percent said it didn't.

That candidate, of course, was Hillary Clinton, at that moment a resident of Washington, D.C., previously a resident of Arkansas and Illinois. She had never lived in New York.

The next poll question rendered a harsher judgment on the First Lady. Fifty-three percent said she didn't "understand the issues and problems" of the state. That was despite several months of campaigning from Canajoharie to

Canarsie, on what had been dubbed Hillary's "listening tour."

Yet there was a pearl in the oyster. The very same Quinnipiac poll showed that voters *did* approve of the way Hillary had presented herself to voters. "Which would you rather see a candidate for the United States Senate spend their time doing," the respondents were asked: "listening to what voters have to say or explaining their positions to voters?" By 54 to 32 percent, people preferred the listener to the explainer.

The "listening tour" idea was working. Rather than start her campaign for the U.S. Senate with an agenda, Hillary Clinton arrived in New York manifesting curiosity. Here was a newcomer eager to listen and learn. She wanted to hear from the people themselves.

The idea had been to play her strengths. Even her worst critics knew Bill Clinton's wife to be brainy, diligent, studious. By taking the humble route, she had also helped erode her negative reputation for being an I-know-best policy wonk. She was already smart, and stopping to "listen" made her seem even smarter.

The strategy was a masterstroke. The people of upstate New York, long ignored by the clamorous politicians of Manhattan, now had someone whose ears were open to them. Evita had come to the mountain.

In fact, Hillary was following not just her husband's wisdom about the value of listening, but also the counsel of the sixteenth-century political maestro Niccolò Machiavelli. He wrote that a prince who has acquired new territories should go and live in them so he can hear of any troubles quickly. "Being on the spot, disorders can be seen as they arise and can be quickly remedied, but living at a distance, they are only heard of when they get beyond remedy."

The combination of Bill Clinton and Niccolò Machiavelli: unbeatable.

Compare this canny political behavior with George W. Bush's failure to pay firsthand, personal, on-the-spot attention to the people of New Orleans in those hideous days just after Hurricane Katrina. While thousands of displaced families were without potable water at the Convention Center, the president was on his ranch in Crawford, Texas. Only after crucial days passed did he catch up on the devastation, from White House–made DVDs of nightly news reports that everyone else in the country had been glued to and left brokenhearted by.

Machiavelli has nothing good to say about such inattention to duty. "The prince who fails to recognize troubles in his state as they arise is not truly wise." I've often wondered how different the history of his presidency would be if Bush had arrived in New Orleans on Marine One personally to hand out water bottles to those desperate people. What if he'd stood there, ignoring all attendant dangers and had instead listened to the abundant needs?

You say it couldn't have worked? Well, I will never forget how stirring it was when this same Bush arrived at the rubble of the World Trade Center four years earlier and stood there, arm in arm, with the firefighters.

Keep in mind that poll number showing that citizens prefer the politician who listens to the one who talks. In the aftermath of the 2004 presidential election, we screened two vignettes from the campaign on *The Chris Matthews Show*. In one we saw John Kerry campaigning in a local diner; in the second we saw his rival, President George W. Bush, in a similar setting.

In the first clip, candidate Kerry is leaning over a young woman who is there having her lunch alone. "Go to my website, JohnKerry.com," Kerry instructs her, "and you'll see my economic plan to protect the middle class, grow jobs, give tax incentives for manufacturing." All very informative but the kind of virtuously educational campaign moment better suited to a League of Women Voters forum than a chat over french fries.

Cut to the scene at another diner. We see President Bush walk through the door and spot a young family crowded around a table. "What an honor to say hello," he says, beaming. "There are three sisters, four sisters," he counts the kids, "and one little dude!" Here's the president of the United States using the encounter not to showcase himself but rather the people whose lives he has dropped in on.

Don't you think those parents are going to remember the president of the United States calling their son "dude"? Isn't it great how Bush instantly sympathized with the kid for being the only boy amid so many girls? Bush's instant appreciation of that kid's situation showed him, for a change, to be truly connected to daily life in this country.

Okay, you can point out that the comparison isn't fair. You can say we're better off—and I would agree—having a candidate with a full-fledged economic plan than one who can breeze his way into a diner.

But focus on what's going on here in human terms. One candidate is showing an interest in a family, and the other is directing interest to his political agenda. Which is more appealing? Which campaigner seemed most genuinely interested in the people he was greeting? Bush appeared to be enjoying his outing to make contact with regular Americans who live beyond the Beltway, while Kerry acted as if he were standing behind a lectern at the Brookings Institution.

People think of politicians as big talkers. The folks who win elections are big *listeners*. They know that the way to a stranger's heart is to display some spark of interest in them. It's not all pretense. The best of them are genuinely curious about other people, including those citizens who can't yet vote. Am I the only parent who judges my fellow adults by how much attention they give my children?

In 2006 we celebrated the start of the fifth season of *The Chris Matthews Show* at the historic Hay-Adams Hotel, overlooking Lafayette Park and the White House. It was a gorgeous late-summer night, and that grand gentleman Senator John Warner of Virginia had joined us out on the balcony. He turned his attention to my seventeen-year-old daughter, who was then deeply caught up in the worries of applying to college.

"So what are you going to do with your life, young lady?"

"I'm thinking of becoming a doctor," Caroline answered in a rare public declaration of her dreams.

"What a *wonderful* way to spend your life," Warner told her warmly. "My father was a doctor."

What a politician. *What* a gentleman. Everyone else is bantering about politics or the news business and he's shown his charm and upbringing by focusing on the dreams of my teenage daughter.

There is nothing so winning as a readiness to listen. People love it. I remember the way my longtime boss Tip O'Neill welcomed my aunt Eleanor, a nun who had spent a half century in a teaching order, with many of those years dedicated to special education.

"So how long have you been out of the habit?" the Speaker asked as he greeted her in his Capitol office. She beamed at him. I can't imagine a better icebreaker for a religious sister who undoubtedly had never forgotten that glorious day she was allowed to forgo that black, starchy, face-squeezing medieval costume.

Listening is what helped Congressman Dick Gephardt of Missouri rise to become the House's Democratic leader. I often watched him hold long meetings of the party's most ambitious members and observed how he would offer everyone a chance to talk, moving the conversation smoothly from one voice to another. He never interrupted with his own view, and instead patiently allowed the less senior members to speak their piece. He was their chosen leader for the very reason that he had proved himself a guarantor that each voting member of the caucus would be given his or her chance to speak.

The first President Bush is another superb listener. Early in 1989, soon after taking office, he invited a small group, my wife and me included, to the White House for dinner and a movie.

Perhaps it was impertinent on my part, but I sent word that my mother and father were set to visit me that night; could I bring them along? The answer quickly came back: President and Mrs. Bush would be pleased to have my parents join them. Herb and Mary Matthews, naturally, were thrilled.

We arrived and soon were being given a quick tour by

First Lady Barbara Bush. Standing in the Truman Building, I remember spotting three people through the French doors chatting merrily away—my parents and the president. During the buffet dinner my dad and I exchanged glances: Yes, this was really happening and he was a guest of the president of the United States—a personal guest.

As we ate, President Bush made a reference to my family being Democrats. It was a reasonable assumption. I had, after all, served as a top aide to Tip O'Neill for six combative years. But the truth was different. So I had to disabuse the president, telling him that, in fact, Dad was a lifelong Republican.

Hearing that, he asked me, without missing a beat, "What happened to you?"

Three months later I was standing in the Roosevelt Room of the White House West Wing. Those of us in the Hearst newspapers' Washington bureau had just had an hourlong briefing by President Bush. About to leave, I saw the president coming around the long table we had all been sitting at, and he was clearly heading for me.

"So has your father changed your mind about things yet?"

More in touch and sharp-witted than people give him credit for, George H. W. Bush remembered I had betrayed my paternal heritage and he couldn't resist scoring a point.

Politicians, the good ones, must excel at the business of people. The best ones listen. They pay attention. They take an interest in other people. With all that ambition festering in their souls, they understand that the realization of it rests on the goodwill, cooperation, and complicity of others.

Think of the people you know who really look into your eyes when you're talking, who seem truly interested in you. Think about the positive response you have to such encounters. If we think about the success of Oprah Winfrey, we realize that there has never been anyone like her for the simple reason that there has never been a popular figure so blessed with the talent for listening to people tell their own stories. It's a power that cuts across lines of race and class and age, this grand capability to lend an attentive, caring ear.

So when you show up for a job interview, don't use up your time talking about what you want. Try to figure out what the interviewer wants.

It's not a bad idea to do this whenever you meet anybody. Try to grasp what the other person has in his or her mind. Make *him* or *her* the subject of the conversation. It's good manners.

Besides, you might learn something.

Bottom Line

It may be a surprising thing to hear from me, the notorious on-air interrupter, but not only is it polite to let people say what they wish to, it's also downright seductive. The best gift you can give is your attention. Believe me, I'm trying to get better at this.

CHAPTER 6

Up Beats Down

*I think the best thing is always to put a good face
upon a disagreeable state of affairs.*
—BENJAMIN DISRAELI

Ya gotta believe!
—TUG MCGRAW

THE FINEST CAMPAIGN POSTER of 2008 America was the color portrait of an upward-looking Barack Obama accompanied by that one, short, inspiring word: *Hope.*

"For many months, we've been teased, even derided for talking about hope," Obama said the night he won the Iowa Democratic Caucuses.

"But we always knew that hope is not a blind optimism. It's not ignoring the enormity of tasks ahead or the roadblocks that stand in our path.

Hope is that thing inside us that insists, despite all the evidence to the contrary, that something better awaits us if we have the courage to reach for it and to work for it and to fight for it."

We Americans are an optimistic people. We respond best to those who speak in our upbeat national idioms.

In July 1979, Jimmy Carter addressed the country on national television. He had just spent more than a week in the woods at Camp David, the presidential retreat. During that time the public was aware that he had summoned there a cross section of prominent Americans for private counsel. Beleaguered by double-digit inflation, high interest rates, long gasoline lines, and low job approval, Carter faced a nation intensely curious to hear what solutions he would have to offer.

Instead, the American president spoke of a "crisis of confidence" racking the country, a crisis of the American "spirit."

"We can see this crisis in the growing doubt about the meaning of our lives and in the loss of a unity of purpose for our nation. The erosion of our confidence in the future is threatening to destroy the social and the political fabric of America," he said.

Carter explained gravely that people no longer felt the certainty that things would get better in America. "We've always believed in something called progress. We have always had faith that the days of our children would be better than our own. Our people are losing faith, not only in government itself but in the ability of citizens to serve as the ultimate rulers and shapers of democracy.

"Our people have turned to the federal government and found it isolated from the mainstream of our nation's life. What you see too often in Washington and elsewhere around the country is a system of government that seems incapable of action."

He quoted one of his recent visitors to Camp David: "We've got to stop crying and start sweating, stop talking and start walking, stop cursing and start praying. The strength we need will not come from the White House, but from every house in America."

The strength we need will not come from the White House. By citing that assessment, Carter was admitting that the American people didn't believe he could lead them. An aide further added to the sense of negativity and pessimism by telling journalists that the theme of Carter's speech was "malaise," a word defined as a "vague awareness of moral or social decline."

The "malaise speech" was followed three days later by Jimmy Carter's call for the resignation of every member of his Cabinet. Though this directive was intended to show resolve—it was followed by five high-level firings—it in fact caused the national mood to deflate even further.

Carter, some argued, had it right. The country *was* in a funk. The political solution, however, was not to make the dismal mood official. Instead of a description of its demoralized conditions, it was obvious that the country wanted a prescription to help cure it.

For Labor Day weekend 1980, now working in the Carter speechwriting shop, I drew the assignment of drafting the president's kickoff for his reelection campaign. Late that holiday Monday, Kathy and I ducked into a Georgetown bar to catch the nightly news and see what kind of coverage the speech, delivered at a big Alabama picnic, had gotten.

Unfortunately, all I recall from that night's broadcast was the sight of our opponent standing in shirtsleeves with

New York Harbor and the Statue of Liberty behind him. Ronald Reagan had rediscovered America's most cinematic, most hopeful icon and was giving it a new soundtrack.

"I'm here because it's the home of Democrats. In this country there are millions of Democrats as unhappy as we are with the way things are going." He spoke movingly of the immigrants who had struggled to reach America. "They didn't ask what this country could do for them but what they could do to make this refuge the greatest home of freedom in history. But today a president of the U.S. would have us believe that dream is over, or at least in need of change."

Carter had gone to great lengths to appraise the situation, only to proclaim, sadly, that the American dream was dead. Now here was his opponent cheerfully promising he would bring it back to life.

One of the strongest advantages the 1980 Republican challenger had on the earnest Democratic incumbent was simply this: Ronald Reagan grasped instinctively how important it was to make Americans feel good about themselves. Carter didn't. More to the point, Ronald Reagan himself believed in the brighter future he spoke of, and his conviction was infectious. Carter, a good and honest man, couldn't stop worrying.

In 2007, a new-generation candidate arrived on the national stage, declaring his presidential candidacy and preaching the gospel of good news. In the language of his father's country *baraka* means "blessed." It describes a person whose mere presence raises everyone's hopes.

Barack Obama had first introduced himself to the country at the 2004 Democratic National Convention.

There, in Boston's FleetCenter, he delivered the most inspiring speech many Americans listening that evening had
ever heard.

"Let's face it," he declared, "my presence on this stage
is pretty unlikely. My father was a foreign student, born and
raised in a small village in Kenya. He grew up herding goats,
went to school in a tin-roof shack. His father—my grandfather—was a cook, a domestic servant to the British. But
my grandfather had larger dreams for his son. Through
hard work and perseverance, my father got a scholarship to
study in a magical place, America, that shone as a beacon of
freedom and opportunity to so many who had come there."

Obama then told how his white American grandfather
had fought in World War II, in "Patton's army," how he had
gone to college on the GI Bill and harbored great dreams
for his daughter.

"My parents shared not only an improbable love; they
shared an abiding faith in the possibilities of this nation.
They would give me an African name, Barack, believing
that in a tolerant America your name is no barrier to success. They imagined me going to the best schools in the
land, even though they weren't rich, because in a gener-
ous America you don't have to be rich to achieve your
potential."

Obama, at that moment not yet elected to the U.S.
Senate, was offering a miraculous gift with those words.
His very presence, along with his manifest confidence, told
a country long whipsawed by race that a child of black and
white parents could offer not just an idea of national unity,
but also shared aspirations. With thoughtful eloquence,
Obama was marrying the immigrant story to the African

American legacy not simply by his genes but by his genius. No wonder the country's youth turned to him as their hope as well as their hero.

Hope. To hear Senator Barack Obama's words from that 2004 speech was to know his story. To know his story is to feel optimism about the direction of our country. Those parents who dreamed of their son going "to the best schools in the land" saw Obama elected president of the *Harvard Law Review*. The young politician who called himself "a black man with a funny name" would win his Senate seat with majorities in white areas of Illinois as well as black.

In his autobiography, *Dreams from My Father,* Obama writes of "America's hunger for an optimistic sign from the racial front." By his birth and his success, and more important, symbolizing his mother's love for his father, he inspires hope for closure of the racial divide that has separated this country since its birth.

What I heard from my mother that day, speaking about my father, was something that I suspect most Americans will never hear from the lips of those of another race, and so cannot be expected to believe might exist between black and white: the love of someone who knows your life in the round, a love that will survive disappointment. She saw my father as everyone hopes at least one other person might see him; she had tried to help the child who never knew him see him in the same way.

Imagine you are headed for a long plane ride. You have a first-class seat to Australia. You are sitting in 1-A. Who do you want sitting in 1-B? Someone who is clearly enjoying the flight or a guy who's worried and miserable?

I can tell you which sort we Americans generally pick as our president.

I was in the House chamber on that night in 1981 when Ronald Reagan came back, Lazarus-like, having survived an assassin's attack. Hardly a month earlier, he'd been at death's door, victim of a close-to-the-heart gunshot wound. "I hope you're all Republicans," he kidded the doctors about to operate at George Washington Hospital. "Honey, I forgot to duck," he told wife Nancy when she reached his bedside.

And now he stood there before the U.S. Congress, ready to pitch his economic plan of tax and spending cuts. But first he told those assembled in the great chamber that he had a letter to read. It had been sent by a boy who wanted the recuperating president to know how worried he was about him. "I hope you get well quick," the young man wrote, "or you might have to make a speech in your pajamas." Everyone had to chuckle along with him. It was an unmistakable Reagan moment. The man was unsinkable, the kind of upbeat president we Americans can't resist, the kind of person most people can't resist.

Years ago, I interviewed a close pal of John F. Kennedy's named Chuck Spalding, who had hung around with the future president starting in the 1940s when both were in their twenties. He remembered being with Kennedy in San Francisco when Jack was there covering the founding conference of the United Nations for Hearst.

It was the late spring of 1945, a difficult period, with

World War II just ended in Europe and the Soviet Union just starting to show its Cold War colors. Everyone understood, including the young JFK, the seriousness of the chess game we were playing.

Yet the weight of the times, which Kennedy reflected in his reports for the *Chicago American* and other newspapers, didn't limit his joy in the occasion.

As Spalding described him there, "Jack's attitude, as it was in so many other crises, made you feel you were at a *fair* or something."

In a similar vein, I remember what my hero Winston Churchill said of his wartime ally Franklin Roosevelt. He said that meeting FDR was "like opening your first bottle of champagne."

Roosevelt had campaigned to "Happy Days Are Here Again" back in 1932, both an upbeat ditty and a bold promise to a country where 25 percent of the people were out of work.

Great politicians sell hope. Three decades later, Jack Kennedy ran to the accompaniment of "High Hopes," the Frank Sinatra hit. If elected, he promised to get the country "moving again." And he did.

During Kennedy's presidency his New Frontier zest inspired young men and women to join the Peace Corps and underpinned his commitment to the space program and putting Americans on the moon. Optimism was the pervasive spirit of his administration, and made the tragedy of his death so stark.

Ronald Reagan came to us with a celluloid version of a presidential campaign. No one was better at evoking that

big-screen bravado of World War II. And when he deci-
sively won his second term, it was with that cowboy grin
declaring it was "morning in America." The sun was just
coming up, and he was urging us to bask in it.

Bill Clinton billed himself as the "man from Hope"—
Arkansas, that is—and ran to the beat of Fleetwood Mac's
"Don't Stop (Thinking About Tomorrow)." "There is nothing wrong with America," he confidently announced, "that
cannot be cured with what is right with America."

Every good leader, whether president or member of the
local town board, knows that the heart of America beats
faster when optimism is being trumpeted. New York governor Mario Cuomo, one of the few great orators in modern
American politics, once confided to me that he always
ended his addresses—even his withering rebuke of Republican economic policies at the Democratic convention in
1984—with a hopeful note.

Researchers at the University of Texas pulled together all
the words spoken by the presidential and vice presidential
candidates in 2004. When they ran them through a com-
puter, the results were telling. The candidates on the Democratic ticket, John Kerry and John Edwards, it turns out,
used more downbeat language than Republican candidates
George W. Bush and Dick Cheney.

"Voters are more favorable toward those candidates
who are the most optimistic," the chief researcher wrote.
"The depressive language that Kerry and Edwards used
during their campaign may have contributed negatively to
the way in which they were perceived by the public." D'ya
think?

Certainly the converse is true. One explanation for the enduring affection of Massachusetts voters for Senator Edward Kennedy is the upbeat spirit he exudes. Here is a man who carries enormous tragedy on his shoulders, including the violent deaths of three older brothers, all killed in the service of their country.

Yet Ted Kennedy embodies the very essence of the United States Senate, not just as a legislator, but as a colleague and, yes, fellow clubman. No matter how serious the moment, he can lift the mood of any event by the sheer strength of his wit and will. Such a gift may well account for his era-spanning senatorial career.

Back in the early 1950s, his older brother John, known for his passion for the lessons of history, was asked to select the four greatest U.S. senators ever. He could, of course, only look backward. Had that first Senator Kennedy been able to look forward, I think he would surely have included his youngest brother. If you don't believe he deserves such distinction, just ask any conservative colleague of his.

Bottom Line

Optimism sells. You can try this one at home: Tell someone close to you that you're feeling positive about some family worry. Don't just hope for good health, happiness, and all the rest. Get out there and *root* for it!

CHAPTER 7

Ask!

*For it is the nature of men to be bound by the benefits
they confer as much as by those they receive.*
—Niccolò Machiavelli

*In politics, strangely enough, the best way to play your cards
is to lay them face upward on the table.*
—H. G. Wells

THE EARLY PHASE OF THE 2008 presidential campaign
taught America a powerful lesson in fund-raising. It
showed how skillful the top politicians have become at so-
liciting contributions. We watched as the top Democratic
contenders, Senators Hillary Clinton and Barack Obama,
battled it out in what was billed "the money primary." We
watched former Massachusetts governor Mitt Romney
amass an early war chest far greater than those of his Republican rivals. That itself shouldn't have surprised us. A
venture capitalist by trade, Romney has spent his career
raising cash.

Politicians have elevated fund-raising to a finely tuned
enterprise. The Obama '08 website offered guidance on

how to "Make Your Donation a Monthly Commitment." The donor was asked to check the box for anywhere from fifty to five hundred dollars a month, then fill in his or her credit card information. It was a state-of-the-art method for exploiting human nature. As veteran fund-raisers know, once a person kicks in the first time, that donor becomes a good bet to give more. It's what makes contributors' lists such a valued campaign asset.

Given the huge rivalry that plays itself out in TV advertising, the ability to convince people to shell out is a candidate's job requirement. No matter how charismatic they are, politicians still must raise vast sums. It's instructive to watch how the best of them do it.

Listen to Senator John McCain, out building early support for 2008. "The good news is we have enough money to fund Dave's campaign," went his seasoned pitch for a local political ally. Then he added the kicker: "The bad news is it's still in your wallets and purses."

What you hear there is the sound of *bonding*. The message is that he and the audience he's pitching are all in it together. He's talking to his listeners like they're already part of the team. These are people who've shown their allegiance by buying tickets to a fund-raiser, and he's saying that the right thing to do is up their investment.

There are two sides to any financial transaction, and a political contribution is no exception. On the one side stands the politician seeking money. He'll be grateful to whoever kicks in. On the other side are the contributors. If they donate money to a candidate, they will become, in their own eyes, not just a partisan but a *friend* of the candidate. They'll root for his or her success, not just in the coming election but, usually, for their entire careers.

This is one of politics' favorite secrets—except that it's the kind that's hiding in plain sight. The person who gives money to a political candidate has what amounts to an intimate involvement with his success. This person becomes the most passionate of cheerleaders. The more he has given, the more committed he becomes.

It wasn't a Democrat or a Republican who uncovered this basic truth about human nature, that the giver becomes more invested than the beneficiary. Machiavelli wrote in *The Prince* that after a city was besieged for many months, after the people had lived through tremendous hardship within the city's walls, after they had suffered horror and hunger in defense of their prince, they were all the more loyal to him. Yes, they felt even *more* bound to him, "looking upon him as under an obligation to them for having sacrificed their houses and estates in his defense." "For it is the nature of men," Machiavelli discovered, "to be bound by the benefits they confer as much as by those they receive."

This knowledge of human nature separates the professionals from the rest of the crowd. Amateurs are afraid to ask for help. They worry about becoming indebted to someone.

But it's like the boss who gives a young person a break. If he's given a first job to a promising employee, he'll most likely want to keep pushing that person along, if only to prove he was right the first time. Contributing to a candidate or cause involves the same kind of relationship. The savvy political fund-raiser knows this and never begs when he asks for money; rather, he simply points out what a good deal the campaign is.

Terry McAuliffe and Ed Gillespie graduated a few years apart from Catholic University in Washington. Both are Irish American, both political, both gifted at making friends and influencing people. Their ambitions are what drove both to the highest levels of their parties. McAuliffe became chairman of the Democratic National Committee, Gillespie chairman of the Republican National Committee.

As glorious as the titles sound, both posts share a common job description: chief fund-raiser. To chair a national political party you need a recognized talent for inducing people—especially *rich* people—to part with their money. Listening to McAuliffe and Gillespie on that all-important detail, you can't tell the difference between the Democrat and the Republican. They both rely on the same tried-and-true method. "You've got to convince people you're going to win," McAuliffe told me. "People always want to be with a winner. People don't want to support a loser."

But that's just for openers. The key here is to engage people in the spirit of partisan competition itself. "You've got to get them excited. I like to get people pumped up," explains McAuliffe.

Ed Gillespie starts with the big picture. "I always try to get people to buy into the vision, how what we're doing with the money is important to the country." He then gives his potential donor the inside perspective. "We need another two million to get up with television in Ohio. I'd like you to help there," he'll say. Revealing such a shortfall or a weak spot is a bonding tactic.

"You've got to give them something tangible, show them that you're not going to piss it away somewhere," he said. "Sometimes I'll lay out a program for direct mail and say how it will get turnout up two percent—but we've got to *pay* for it! A lot of people have the money to give. They're successful people. But they want to see results."

McAuliffe, who started as a 1980 reelection fund-raiser for Jimmy Carter within a year of getting out of college, explains that wealthy givers are easier to pitch. "I'd rather ask a person used to giving $100,000 or $200,000. Ask for the big money because the people you're dealing with are used to it. They expect it. They want to see the game. They want to see *how* you're playing it."

The same holds true when it comes to enlisting the loyalties of the not-so-rich. The Kennedy family, for example, has long known the power of passionate campaign volunteers. Starting with Jack Kennedy's first campaign for Congress in 1946, the idea was to sign up every volunteer you could. It didn't matter if a person was just stopping by the headquarters; they might be recruited if only to write personal thank-you notes on behalf of the Kennedy family to others who had stopped by.

The trick was to get them doing *something, anything,* that turned them into "Kennedy volunteers." Once these new foot soldiers started sharing their enthusiasm, their neighbors would want to come on board, too. In this way, it soon became a communal experience that motivated people and cemented loyalties.

Jimmy Carter was a nobody to most people when he

began his improbable campaign for president. In opinion polls taken in late 1975 and early 1976, his name didn't even register. His only—not very compelling—claim on the nation's attention was his single term as Georgia governor. Yet on his side was his audacity, the ability to declare himself and ask for support.

What did he have to lose? "I'm Jimmy Carter and I'm running for president." With those words, he began a coast-to-coast campaign, the snowball effect of which defeated the established Democratic candidates and swept out a sitting president. Since some Democrat was likely to win the presidency in the aftermath of the Watergate scandal, Carter had decided it might as well be him.

And Jimmy Carter had other ploys. For example, he'd stay at people's houses rather than at a nearby hotel. The gift of a bed became his host's intimate bond with the campaign. As former John Kennedy aide Ted Sorensen, then supporting the Georgia governor, observed, "How can you vote against someone after they've slept on your couch?"

The politician teaches us to benefit from an important aspect of human nature: The more a person invests in you, the greater the bond. Don't be afraid to ask people to buy your product or invest in your enterprise. You're not begging. Remember, you're giving them a chance at the action. There's something in it for them.

The key is to realize that what you're really offering is a chance to be involved.

Try this yourself. Imagine that you're running in an election for president of your class or social group. To win, designate a number for each person in the group. Give a

1 to all your friends, a 2 to people you regularly say hi to but don't consider that close, a 3 to people you feel are probably truly undecided about you, and a 4 to those you figure are either strongly against you or loyal to another candidate.

Here's your campaign: Approach those you've given the number 1 to and say that you know you're friends but that you're asking them to vote for you. This should nail down your base. Then approach each of those you've tagged with a 2 and make your basic campaign pitch. Tell them what your plans are if elected and how you believe you can really do the job. Ask them for their vote. The important thing with this group is to treat them as people you have to convince. They will appreciate your direct, positive, respectful approach. Finally, go to the people you've marked with a 3 and give them an aggressive, extensive case for your election. They are the persuadables—so persuade them! Do not approach the people you categorized with the number 4. It'll only get them aroused. If you bump into them, just be friendly, noncon-frontational, and dull. Any active campaigning will simply provoke them. You want them to go to sleep.

The most vital category of voters for you are the 1's. When my boss Tip O'Neill ran for the Cambridge city council back in the 1930s, the woman living across the street complained later that O'Neill, still at Boston College, hadn't bothered to ask for her vote. "People like to be *asked*," she said. Tip O'Neill lost that race but never another.

This numbering system has been proven in many a successful campaign. It's based on the principle that people generally stick to their word and that they *all* like to be asked. Believe me, it'll work for you.

Bottom Line

When you set out to raise money, win votes, whatever involves getting people to say yes, don't think about your end of the deal. Focus on why a person should contribute. Explain clearly and boldly how it will give them an investment in the effort, an in-the-know role in the operation, make them a real player in the enterprise.

CHAPTER 8

Don't Call Just When You Need Something

Dig your well before you're thirsty.
—HARVEY MACKAY

*If you live in the river, you should make friends
with the crocodile.*
—INDIAN PROVERB

P RESIDENT GEORGE HERBERT WALKER BUSH knew how
to build a posse. When he took America to war with
Iraq that first time, back in 1991, we didn't go alone. We
had the British, the French, and the Arab League on our
side of the war. We had the Germans and the Japanese to
help pick up the tab. In other words, we had a leader who
knew the value of allies in a fight.

The son of a Connecticut senator, Bush had served two
terms in the House of Representatives, where he made lifelong friends on both sides of the aisle, treasuring his mem-
bership in that bipartisan club. He also had diplomatic
experience, having served as America's ambassador to the
United Nations and as our envoy to the People's Republic

of China. Moreover, as a former CIA director, he had valuable personal connections in the Middle East.

That first Bush to occupy the White House brought something else to Pennsylvania Avenue with him: a way of seeing other nations that involved respect. Having shipped out to fight in World War II at the age of eighteen, he wrote home that he couldn't buy into the "Kill the Japs" propaganda being put out by our government. "All the well-educated fellows know what they are fighting for," he explained in a letter to his mother, "and don't need to be brainwashed."

Just as important, the man who led us to victory in the Persian Gulf War, boosting American prestige in the process, has always grasped the power of simple courtesy. Famous for writing personal notes to people, he makes relationships, then pays attention to maintaining them.

No sooner was he inaugurated, in 1989, than he took the time to attend the funeral of the Japanese emperor, the one whose planes had shot Bush down in the war. Moreover, though his predecessor, Ronald Reagan, had rather too obviously preferred the company of British prime minister Margaret Thatcher, when it came time to hanging out with foreign pols Bush made sure he gave quality time to Chancellor Helmut Kohl. Such attention to Japan and Germany would matter when America needed rich friends.

George H. W. Bush understood what every Capitol Hill lobbyist knows: You don't just show up when you want something. And such methods made a difference when it came to waging the Persian Gulf War.

Picture this: It's a late afternoon in 1981, Bush's first year as vice president. His press secretary, Peter Teeley, asks the appointments secretary where he might find the boss. It turns out he's home at the vice president's mansion on Massachusetts Avenue "having coffee with the vice president of Egypt."

"Who's he?" Teeley recalls asking impatiently. Why did Bush want to waste the afternoon chatting with a second-level official of a third-world country? Didn't a vice president of the United States have better things to do?

That October, Egyptian president Anwar Sadat would be assassinated by Islamic fundamentalists, and Egypt's number two man, Hosni Mubarak, would become its number one man. Sadat, the sole Arab leader with the courage to make peace with Israel, was being succeeded by a strong pro-Western lieutenant, one who had once enjoyed a private coffee with a new American vice president.

As I mentioned, in early 1989, President Bush, hardly a month in office, had confounded some White House watchers when he chose to drop everything and travel to the other side of the planet to attend the funeral of Emperor Hirohito.

But Bush did more than attend the old emperor's funeral. While in Tokyo, he began a full-fledged courtship of Japan's new prime minister, Toshiki Kaifu. Back home, he hosted his new pal at the White House, held meetings with him in Palm Springs and New York. To the Japanese, such a personal relationship with the American president was a significant enhancer of their prime minister's prestige, and Bush understood this as well.

It paid off. When the Persian Gulf War broke out, Prime Minister Kaifu convinced his Cabinet to join the trade embargo against Iraq. Later, this same Japanese government would contribute $10 billion to the war effort.

But not just attending a funeral was important to the outcome of the Persian Gulf War. Sharing a baseball game was, too.

It's the Orioles versus the Red Sox on the opening day of the American League's 1989 baseball season. In a skybox high above third base in Memorial Stadium, the widow of the Orioles' late owner, Edward Bennett Williams, is hosting a small party for Eli Jacobs, the man who has just bought the team. Among the guests: former Red Sox great Ted Williams, Secretary of State Jim Baker, President George H. W. Bush, and a third-world leader whom the old Yale (1948) team captain made feel very much at home. Bush's guest of honor kept saying how great it was to be there "with one of the world's great baseball players." (He was referring to his presidential host, not Ted Williams.) The two statesmen were given a large basket of baseballs, the idea being that both leaders would sign each one. The signature joining Bush's on the forty-plus souvenir baseballs was that of Hosni Mubarak, the president of Egypt.

Like every player and coach on the Orioles that afternoon, George Bush was a man at work. The home team had a job to do, and so did the sixty-four-year-old in the skybox.

Remember that coffee at the vice president's residence eight years earlier? Now George H. W. Bush wanted to show this ally, one that he had befriended when it wasn't a sure thing, that he was a president of the United States who considered him and his country, Egypt, important—very important. People close to Bush say a great deal of thinking and craft go into such power friendships. "It's important to the way he governs and the way he relates to other nations and their problems," longtime aide and friend Vic Gold told me.

"If you want to understand George Bush the diplomat, look at George Bush the politician," he said. "It's the same modus operandi. He regards politics as person to person. He goes out and works his ass off networking and people-izing. He doesn't start with a policy relationship; he establishes a personal relationship."

In other words, here was a president who could call his fellow world leaders his friends. Toshiki Kaifu, Hosni Mubarak, even France's aloof president François Mitterrand had become people he could get on the line quickly, allies who were willing to give him the benefit of the doubt, and act cooperatively in a crisis.

This is what remains, even today, so breathtaking about the Persian Gulf War. For the first time since the 1940s, the phrase "United Nations" wasn't just an ideal. "He'd established relations with all of these leaders in such a way that his diplomatic efforts were almost on automatic pilot," recalled Pete Teeley. "He just had to reach out and put the pieces in place."

Bush didn't have to reach far.

It is the day of Iraq's invasion of Kuwait: August 2, 1990. Bush and Britain's Margaret Thatcher both happen to be attending a conference at the Aspen Institute. There, in Colorado, the Anglo-American alliance is struck on the spot.

Eight days later, thanks to Egypt's Mubarak, the Arab League votes economic sanctions against Iraq and to send a pan-Arab military force to join in the coalition against Saddam. The next morning, Mubarak gets a call from the White House. Up before dawn, his friend George Bush wants to thank him for his masterful leadership.

Bush's wartime Persian Gulf choreography was not some

dance he had learned for the occasion, but rather the same *retail* politics he'd been practicing for decades with his Cabinet and staff, the White House press corps, and Congress.

One more anecdote: When James Baker was still Treasury secretary, he kept a snapshot on his wall of an embarrassed George Bush taken just seconds after a fall at a bowling alley. The inscription read:

> *To Jim Baker,*
> *Watch and learn: 90 percent of life*
> *is just showing up.*
> *—George Bush*

Woody Allen may have said it, but here was a fellow who lived it.

The lesson we get from the first President Bush is to spend your time investing in *people*. Don't wait till you need friends. Make them when you *can*.

Whatever the arena, nothing builds confidence like the knowledge that there are people you can call in a crunch, people you know from instinct will care about your predicament and come to your aid.

Bottom Line

Don't just call when you need something. If you plan someday to make a withdrawal, it's a good policy to start putting something in the bank. That goes for money, but it goes double for friendship. Wishing won't do it; saving will.

CHAPTER 9

People Don't Mind Being Used; They Mind Being Discarded

A man who has friends must show himself friendly.
—PROVERBS

If you don't go to other people's funerals, they won't go to yours.
—YOGI BERRA

THERE'S A REASON politicians attend funerals. Former New York City mayor Rudolph Giuliani puts it this way: "Weddings are discretionary; funerals are mandatory." It's a code of behavior learned from his Brooklyn bartender father, who took him along to wakes and funerals when he was a boy. As mayor, Giuliani made it his goal to attend the funeral of anyone who had died in the line of duty in New York City.

Even when the World Trade Center attack made that standard impossible to keep, he remained steadfast in his dedication to honoring the dead. "Funerals are difficult. That's why one's needed," Giuliani has written. "And why it means more when one shows up. When the chips are down—when someone you care about is struggling for answers or burying a loved one—that's when the measure of a leader is taken."

But it is equally important to pay one's respects to the living. Handle your allies with the care they deserve. People don't mind being used; they mind being discarded. He who denies that powerful truth should recall the old friends who have done it to *him*. How about the guy who takes a woman on a date and never calls her again? Or the person you once hired for a big job and who later in the game can't remember your name?

Politicians know the price that's paid every time they slip and forget a loyalist's name. Not every supporter expects a Cabinet job or an ambassadorship. A contributor or campaign worker may forgive you for not getting their name right the first or second time but will become openly angry if you never get it straight.

Savvy politicians know how to maintain healthy relations with their backers. Members of Congress send out regular newsletters, hold reunions for volunteers, maintain massive Christmas card lists. They know how people value souvenirs of the political wars that carry forward the sense of shared effort. Such tokens of esteem are the tangible forget-me-nots that cut past otherwise foggy memories of a large ballroom, noisy people, and forgotten speeches.

Rare is the political supporter who doesn't display the framed, autographed picture with the candidate. Jack Kennedy loyalists would sport their *PT-109* tie clasps for decades after the 1960 campaign, enduring evidence of their own close encounter with Camelot.

Never underestimate the power of such trinkets. Remember the story of my initiation as a campaign worker out in Utah? If you visit my house, you'll find a treasured souvenir of the Wayne Owens congressional race of 1972 sitting on my desk. It's a bronze paperweight in the shape of the state on which is inscribed WE WALKED. WE WORKED. WE WON. It's a rugged little memorial to a moment when a little-known candidate from southern Utah made his name by crossing the state on foot. It's also a sweet reminder to me of how it all started.

In February 2007 *The Washington Post* ran a series of muckraking articles exposing the poor treatment accorded the Iraq War wounded at Walter Reed Army Medical Center. Public outrage at accounts of moldy, rat-infested wards and bureaucratic dysfunction was instant. Americans were divided over the wisdom of the war, but they proved to be united in concern for the warriors.

Within days of the shocking revelation, Walter Reed's top officials were fired and the Pentagon had set about making long-overdue repairs to the facilities. Americans are willing to see their young and brave sent into harm's way; they can't stand seeing them betrayed. It's a thousand times worse when the overlooked and undervalued have fought and suffered serious, too often permanent, wounds for their country.

Tip O'Neill, at heart an old street-corner politician all his days, used to recite Henson Towne's poem on the subject. He liked to remind people of the horrors of discarded friendship.

Around the corner I have a friend,
In this great city that has no end,
Yet the days go by and weeks rush on,
And before I know it, a year is gone.

And I never see my old friend's face,
For life is a swift and terrible race,
He knows I like him just as well,
As in the days when I rang his bell.

And he rang mine but we were younger then,
And now we are busy, tired men.
Tired of playing a foolish game,
Tired of trying to make a name.

"Tomorrow" I say! "I will call on Jim
Just to show that I'm thinking of him,"
But tomorrow comes and tomorrow goes,
And distance between us grows and grows.

Around the corner—yet miles away,
"Here's a telegram sir," "Jim died today."
And that's what we get and deserve in the end.
Around the corner, a vanished friend.

Bottom Line

Politics teaches the importance of keeping in touch with old allies. We all need the help of others in life. Most people simply want to be remembered.

Rivalry

CHAPTER 10

Grin When You Fight

I like a man who grins when he fights.
—WINSTON CHURCHILL

Not after six. The Speaker says that here in Washington
we're all friends after six.
—RONALD REAGAN

THIS IS MY OWN FAVORITE LESSON from the great politicians. Even when things get hot, keep your wits about you. Even if the other guy goes after you, don't let it get personal.

The anecdote about that *Hardball* interview with Georgia senator Zell Miller at the Republican National Convention of 2004 I showcased to open the book is a good example. Miller was so overheated that night that he threatened me with a *duel*. Thanks to my MSNBC colleagues, to whom I was listening through my earpiece, I stayed cool. The more the Georgia senator growled, the wider I grinned.

Again, here's the scene: It's a hot summer night in New York. I'm broadcasting from the middle of Herald Square, with Broadway traffic rushing in both directions, and a big loud crowd cheering all around me. Miller, a disgruntled Democrat, has just roundly lambasted Democratic presidential nominee John Kerry in a speech to the roar of the Republican delegates. Pleased with himself, he's now on the big screen in front of me, spoiling for a fight.

"I want to ask you about the most powerful line in your speech, and it had so many," I began. "Do you believe that John Kerry and Ted Kennedy *really* only believe in defending America with spitballs?"

"Well, I certainly don't believe they want to defend America by putting the kind of armor and the kind of equipment that they have got to have out there."

"I'm just asking you, Senator, do you mean to say—I know there's rhetoric in campaigns—that you *really* believe that John Kerry and Ted Kennedy do not believe in defending the country?"

"Wait a minute. I didn't say . . . I didn't question their patriotism."

"Do you believe that they don't believe in defending the country," I pressed.

"I question their judgment," he answered.

Now came his first warning shot.

"I want to be as nice as I possibly can to you," he said. "I wish I was over there, where I could get a little closer *up into your face*." The crowd around me on Broadway, listening on speakers, started to go crazy.

Miller's temperature was obviously rising. "I knew you were going to be coming with all of that stuff. That's just baloney. You've got to quit taking those Democratic talking points."

"No, I'm using *your* talking points and asking you if you really *believe* them," I said.

"I think we ought to cancel this interview," Miller snapped.

By now the crowd is really roaring. My executive producer, Tammy Haddad, is, as usual, in my ear, connected to me by earpiece. But the voice I'm hearing now is that of Rick Kaplan, president of MSNBC.

"Savor it," Rick encourages me, excitedly hoping I won't let the fish off the hook. "Stretch it out." The veteran Kaplan knows the weird symbiosis that lets viewers know there's something wild happening on another network and to go searching for it.

"Well, that would be my loss, Senator," I responded to my guest's threat to split. "That would be my loss," I repeated—and I *meant* it.

Next I asked the senator why he had just said in his speech that it's "not the reporter" who fights for freedom of the press but the "soldier." Was that, I inquired, just "an applause line against the media at a conservative convention"? In other words, a cheap shot?

"You're hopeless," Miller shot back. "I wish I was over there . . . I wish we still lived in the day . . ."

Here it comes.

"I've got to warn you," I interrupted him. "We are in a tough part of town over here. But I recommend you come over because I like you." Okay, now I was teasing him.

"You know, I wish we lived in the day where you could challenge a man to a duel. Now that would be pretty good."

Ignoring such a bizarre escalation of the interview, I extended instead my network's hospitality. Both NBC and I would welcome him.

"Can you come over? I need you, Senator. Please come over."

"You get in my face. I'm going to get back in your face," he retorted.

"You can help our ratings tremendously if you come over tomorrow night because everybody thinks you are going to beat me up." I was speaking for the team at this point, imagining the Nielsen numbers.

When I look back at the videotape of this startling encounter, I'm the one smiling, while Zell Miller, Democratic hero of the GOP convention, is hovering at the boiling point. I now call that September night in 2006 my own personal "Miracle on 34th Street." It's what *Hardball* is all about: We're in the middle of the action, where the questions are tough, and we can provide the unexpected and mesmerizing spectacle of a politician going ballistic.

TV Guide later included the Matthews-Miller bout in its most "unexpected moments" in television history. For weeks afterward, *Saturday Night Live* kept sketches coming that poked fun at the vein-in-his-forehead-popping Zell Miller. But it took me until the next day to realize what a big night it had been for our show and what an unforgettable political moment it was.

In the first hours after we signed off, I must confess I was worried that Miller was serious, or even semi-serious. I insisted that my producers resist any high-fives around town that night. I didn't want to end up at dawn on some grassy field standing at fifty paces being offered my choice of Confederate pistols.

Here's what I wrote in my notes when I got back to my hotel:

> Thursday 2 A.M.
> Wild, strange, almost nasty interview with Zell Miller tonight. He jumped back when I questioned his case that John Kerry voted against all weapons and would have our forces fight with "spitballs." He said that was a metaphor. A metaphor for what, I asked. He proposed a "duel."
> We'll see what way this thing goes.

It wasn't until I got a call the next day from Governor Arnold Schwarzenegger of California, who had himself delivered a boffo speech to the 2004 Republican convention, that I fully grasped the national verdict. "That man's a moron!" Schwarzenegger delightedly declared. "He gave you a million dollars in publicity! He should be having lunch with you right now, making peace."

I've learned to relish such skirmishes. They come with the territory. It's freewheeling political debate that makes our country great. Democracy is supposed to be noisy. If we ever get all calm and cozy on our debate, I'll begin to worry. Next time you see me grinning in a highly charged *Hardball* moment, you'll know why.

I met Ronald Reagan personally for the first time in early 1982. It was in Room 209 of the U.S. Capitol, Speaker O'Neill's ceremonial office, which was the president's usual "holding room" for such occasions. In a few minutes he'd be addressing the U.S. Congress, the American people, and the world. Until then, the Secret Service would keep him in Room 209 while the dogs sniffed for bombs under the seats on the House floor. "Welcome, Mr. President, to the room where we plot against you!" I said upon entering.

"Not after six," our guest responded without hesitation. "The Speaker says that here in Washington we're all friends after six!"

Yes, it really happened that way. I was that impudent and Ronald Reagan that adroit with his comeback.

What I didn't know then was these two men already shared a private interlude in history that few were aware of. When President Reagan had been shot in the spring of 1981, few outside his immediate circle realized how close he had actually come to death, and his chief of staff, James Baker, aware of the president's critical state, was determined to give his boss the rest he needed for recovery.

While the president was recuperating at George Washington University Hospital, Baker had chief White House lobbyist Max Friedersdorf stand guard at the executive bedside specifically to keep away any big-shot visitors who tried talking their way in to see him. But the first person Baker permitted to visit Reagan was Speaker Tip O'Neill.

"So Tip came down," Friedersdorf recalled. "And it was rather poignant. I stayed in the room. Tip got down on his knees next to the bed and said a prayer for the president and he held his hand and kissed him and they said a prayer together. One about, what is it? 'Walking by still waters,' the psalm."

It was the 23rd Psalm. "The Lord is my shepherd. I shall not want . . ."

"The Speaker stayed there quite a while," Friedersdorf said. "They never talked too much. I just heard him say the prayer, then I heard him say, 'God bless you, Mr. President, we're all praying for you.' The Speaker was crying. The president still, I think, he was obviously sedated, but I think he knew it was the Speaker because he said, 'I appreciate you coming down, Tip.' He [O'Neill] held his hand, sat there by his bed and held his hand for a long time."

I like to think back on that picture of simple humanity. One man in crisis, the other praying for him. I recall, too, Reagan's assessment of O'Neill that he inserted in his diary the night of March 17, 1983, after attending a St. Patrick's Day lunch given by the Speaker. "Tip is a true *pol*. He can really like you personally and be a friend while politically trying to beat your head in."

For six years I stood at Tip O'Neill's side as he challenged Reagan on issue after issue, and though he never mentioned that moment, there was something grand about their rivalry. I think it made both of them—and the country—the better for it.

As I came to know him, Ronald Reagan was a tougher, more on-guard character than one would assume from his breezy public personality. He was a combatant who knew, without needing a warning, just when he had entered the enemy's lair. But he understood not to take those political fights personally. If you watch his debates with Jimmy Carter and Tip O'Neill and all the others, you'll definitely see a man who could *grin* when he fought.

Every politician must understand in his or her bones that opposition in life comes on a daily basis. You hold one position, someone else holds a different one. You want to prevail, and so do your rivals, who, if you give it any thought, have just as much right to their attitudes and ambitions as you do.

Besides, when confronting a tough opponent, the best weapon often turns out to be laughter. I think of candidate Jack Kennedy speaking about Richard Nixon in Wichita Falls, Texas, just a few days before they faced each other in the 1960 election.

"In 1951 Nixon called Truman a traitor. In 1960 he called me a liar. In 1960 he called Lyndon an ignoramus. Lyndon said he called me one. I said he called *him* one. He called *me* rash, inexperienced, reckless and uninformed. But he called Lyndon an ignoramus," Kennedy said.

A day later in Toledo, Kennedy kept it up. "In the last four days he has called me everything from a barefaced liar to an economic ignoramus."

The day after that, in the Bronx, Kennedy said that Nixon had called him "an economic ignoramus, a Pied Piper and all the rest. I just confine myself to calling him a Republican. But he says that is *really* getting low."

Kennedy was the *best*.

You gain more by engaging someone with gusto than by taking it personally. Remember the words of Richard Nixon the day he left the White House in shame: "Those who hate you don't win unless you hate them, and then you destroy yourself." When it was all too late, after Watergate and all the rest, he *got* it. He finally *got* it!

Sometimes the hardest thing to do is to look your rival in the face and chat casually. As Tip O'Neill's trusted chief counsel Kirk O'Donnell used to say: Being willing to talk gives you the edge. And guess what? You might even learn something.

More important, never stop trying to see things from the other guy's side. This will help to keep the rivalry in perspective.

Bottom Line

Whatever the race, whatever the prize, *relish* the *contest* and respect your rival, if only for having the good judgment in life to want the same reward you want. And when the moment comes to you, *grin*. It delights the crowd and drives your opponent *nuts*.

CHAPTER 11

It's Not Crowded at the Top

The best reason to have an office in the West Wing
is that you get to piss next to H. R. Haldeman.
—DANIEL PATRICK MOYNIHAN
on the power of
President Nixon's dictatorial chief of staff

Location, location, location.
—REAL ESTATE MOTTO

*T*HE WEST WING was a great, often stirring television series. Every week it put on display the two strongest emotions felt by young staffers working at the White House: personal loyalty to the president and a daily reverence for that unique workplace.

I knew both well. My job as a speechwriter for President Carter was one of the greatest joys of my life. Like everyone else there, I especially loved eating lunch at the White House mess, often at the round table where you grabbed a seat among other staffers and shared the daily scuttlebutt.

I recall with fondness walking the long outdoor corridor that runs from the West Wing to the White House basement, with its scent of rhododendron. Then came that long hallway beneath the Executive Mansion itself where you are surrounded by portraits of presidents and First Ladies.

The West Wing captured that sense, which I personally experienced, of youth confronting history, of gung ho staffers putting their hearts into their work. As viewers of this series sensed, the fictional characters represented those real-life young men and women engaged in what might be the one great moment of their lives, the chance to serve a president of the United States and participate in that grand, high-stakes endeavor of leading the country.

The timing of The West Wing was also critical to its success. The show hit the air just as the country was recoiling from the Monica mess. Bill Clinton had embarrassed friends and empowered enemies by lying under oath about his relationship with a young staffer. The misconduct reminded Americans—those for and against him—of the reverence we hold for this house we built for our presidents.

Yet, despite its on-the-mark evocation of what it's like working for the president, there was one profound inaccuracy in The West Wing: the traffic. In scene after scene, one saw troops of unnamed people walking through the room. Again and again, the main actors managed crises as an endless parade of extras marched past.

In the real West Wing, the hallways are quiet. Only rarely do you pass someone. The offices are small and there are just enough of them to house the most important people: the vice president, the chief of staff, the top aides for national security and domestic policy, the press secretary, and his shop. That's it. All that bustle and traffic you see on the TV version must have been borrowed from its prime-time cousin *ER*. Whatever else it is, the president's work-place is not a big-city hospital emergency room.

The White House's real West Wing is set up to give America's leader the small number of advisors he needs close at hand—and no more. The design, in fact, might be called Machiavellian, for five centuries ago the brilliant Florentine himself laid the intellectual groundwork for such a floor plan, warning the princes of his day to avoid two opposing dangers.

One is *flattery,* the kind that comes from advisors afraid to tell you the hard, often difficult facts. The second is *hu-miliation,* a situation that might arise from an inner circle that's gotten too crowded. Machiavelli said a prince should surround himself with a small select group of advis-ors, letting them and *only* them speak candidly to him.

The West Wing is small, therefore, because it is in the interest of the president that it be so. Around him should be only those he can trust to honor his cause, keep his secrets, and protect him from his faults as well as his enemies.

To make things cozy in the West Wing, presidents keep the bulk of their support team over at the giant Executive Office Building. As one of President Carter's speechwrit-ers, I had a large cube of an office in the EOB. And the greater influence and prestige of those who worked in more confined quarters across the walkway in the West Wing was always clear to us.

The design and utility of the West Wing shows it's not meant to be crowded at the top. Only a select few get to work there.

Jim Baker was the preeminent White House chief of

staff of modern times. He helped Ronald Reagan become a successful president not by "letting Reagan be Reagan," but by helping his boss do the things he most needed and wanted to do in the limited time he had. Baker directed the brilliant victory of the Reagan tax cuts, budget shifts, and military buildups—in other words, the legislative triumphs that defined the fortieth president's term.

Just as important, he kept his boss "on message," as they like to say in Washington. Every cabdriver in America knew that Ronald Reagan wanted to defeat the Soviet Union by outspending it on strategic weaponry and that he wanted to cut the size of government by cutting its tax base. The public knew this precisely because of Baker's ability to manage the focus and energies of the president he served.

It wasn't until Baker left early in the second term to become secretary of the Treasury that things started to go wrong. The debacle of the Iran-Contra scandal demonstrated what happens when management isn't doing its job. It's hard to imagine such a stunt—selling weapons to hostile Iran, sending the profits to Nicaraguan rebels—passing muster under Baker's watch.

Hiring Baker had been a brilliant stroke by President Reagan and one encouraged by his wife, Nancy. The fact that Baker had worked to deny Reagan the presidency twice, managing campaigns for both Gerald Ford and George H. W. Bush, mattered little. What did count were his considerable skills.

Having won the election, Reagan knew he needed the effectiveness of a Jim Baker to exploit the victory. A trained actor and television host, Ronald Reagan understood his strengths and knew his role. He also knew there had to be an experienced director to keep him on script, maintain continuity, and keep the drama of his presidency sharply focused.

Jim Baker relished the power he had been given while never forgetting who had given it to him. He knew, too, that "proximity" is power in the White House: He understood that when a president asks, "What do you think?" it is the staff that answers, not members of the Cabinet or U.S. senators.

I watched up close how Baker did his job. Each time President Reagan made a key decision involving the Congress, his chief of staff would ask for a private visit with Tip O'Neill. Jim Baker would travel across town to the Hill without the press or other politicians knowing it. He would meet with the Speaker in a quiet, out-of-the-way room and give him a heads-up on what the president was planning to do. In this regard, he proved the perfect diplomat, always respecting the protocols, always paying tribute to the office of the Speaker even as he was strategizing the partisan assault on its occupant.

It was an elegant performance: respectful, tough, professional. If the man was this careful honoring the elected leader of Congress, it said a lot to me about how he respected the office of the president. Despite his elite background, Jim Baker never confused his role with that of the constitutional principals. This was his craft, and also his statement as a public servant.

Who's in the room? This is my favorite political question. When all hell breaks loose, whom does a leader call into the room to be there beside him? Whom does he or she trust for the toughest, best advice when the options are awful and the solutions elusive? Fortunately for the Reagan presidency, especially in that crucial first year that saw both an attempted assassination and significant legislative achievement, Jim Baker was in the room.

George W. Bush has not been so fortunate. He selected as his vice president the very same man he had enlisted to help him search for and choose his administration's vice president. That says it all. Thus, Dick Cheney, a former congressman, leader in the House of Representatives, and secretary of defense, convinced the younger Bush he himself was the best choice, setting the stage for him to become the most powerful vice president in history.

Cheney's strength is his bulldog pleasure in a fight. Yet in his role as Bush's top deputy, pugnacity posed an occupational danger. Rather than refine his boss's impulses, as Baker had done for the first Bush, Cheney encouraged the son to cross boundaries. Where Bush needed discretion—in assaying the evidence of Saddam Hussein's nuclear potential, in confronting the consequences of an Iraq invasion *up front*—Cheney was worse than useless. Rather than temper President Bush's urge to attack, he loudly blew the bugle.

Dick Cheney had returned to public office in 2001 with a mission of his own, a desire to topple Saddam Hussein, something he and Bush's father had decided *against* doing in the Persian Gulf War. He was now a deputy with a dangerous agenda of his own.

Because it's not crowded at the top, a few people, those in the room with the leaders, possess a vital power. A prince, Machiavelli wrote, needs to be an "extensive questioner" of those around him, and "should even show his anger in case anyone should, for some reason, not tell him the truth." George W. Bush never thought to ask the tough questions before attacking Iraq, and since Dick Cheney and his fellow hawks were themselves so primed to send in the troops, they were hardly going to raise them.

That's not how it's supposed to work.

It's not crowded at the top. Think about your own workplace. Who gets invited to meet with the boss? Who doesn't? Who's in the loop? Who can tell you what's really happening? It's worth remembering the instructions Franklin Roosevelt once gave his most trusted aide, Harry Hopkins, when he sent him on a mission to wartime London to get a fix on the influences on Prime Minister Winston Churchill: "Find out the men he sees after midnight." It was exactly the right question to ask, and told him everything he needed to know about the man championing Great Britain through its "finest hour."

A legendary presidential counselor, Clark Clifford, once described to me what it was like to sit in a meeting with John F. Kennedy. His stirring account dramatizes how any first-rate president must deal with his advisors.

Clifford, the aide credited with helping Harry Truman pull off his upset electoral victory in 1948, told of one day sitting with Kennedy at the Cabinet table. Watching the president, he imagined his mind rising high above the advisors he'd assembled, listening to every point of view offered, and—with total ruthlessness—deciding what was in the interest of *John F. Kennedy.*

Yet it's what a leader must do, since all advice is multi-layered. They must separate out their advisors' purposes from what is useful to their own.

Bottom Line

"It's not crowded at the top" conveys not just a political fact of life, but a useful truth whatever your interest—a job application, a promotion, a sale, college admission. The best question any insider can answer for you is, "Who's in the room?" Who's there when the boss makes the big decision? Whom does he call into the room? Know that and you know where power lies.

CHAPTER 12

No One's Ever Late for an Execution

In Italy, for thirty years under the Borgias,
they had warfare, terror, murder, bloodshed—
they produced Michelangelo, Leonardo da Vinci, and the Renaissance.
In Switzerland, they had brotherly love,
five hundred years of democracy and peace,
and what did they produce? The cuckoo clock.
—from the film THE THIRD MAN

Whenever a friend succeeds, a little something in me dies.
—GORE VIDAL

POLITICIANS KNOW WHAT IT'S LIKE to face opposition. Unlike amateurs, seasoned professionals can handle knowing someone is gunning for them. Competition for position, as I've said, is the business they've *chosen.* They realize when they awake each morning that there's an ambitious person out there—perhaps more than one—who's begun his day with an eye on their job. Rivalry, *zero-sum* rivalry, comes with the territory.

Ronald Reagan loved telling the story of the guy who was out camping with a friend one night and awoke to see him frantically shoving on his sneakers.

"What are you doing?" he asked.

"There's a bear outside!" his terrified companion exclaimed.

"You can't outrun a bear," the first fellow pointed out.

"No!" yelled his pal, darting from the tent. "But I can outrun *you!*"

In the times I was in the same room with him, as I said, President Reagan's personality surprised me. Expecting to meet a Jimmy Stewart character, a smiling, easygoing fellow, instead I saw more of a Jimmy Cagney type, wary, even edgy, a political combatant very much aware of the predators about him, always on guard against his enemies.

Dave Powers, who traveled the 1960 presidential campaign trail with John F. Kennedy, had a neat ploy for getting his candidate out of bed in the morning: He'd sweep open the curtains, bathing his young hero in sunlight, all the while bantering about what Kennedy rival Richard Nixon had been up to that morning. "I wonder how many factory gates Nixon has been at this morning *already.* I wonder how many key people he's met."

No, but he can outrun you.

Politicians instinctively know the truth others try not to face: that every victory by the other guy is a loss for you. "I don't mind not being president," Ted Kennedy said after losing his intraparty challenge to President Jimmy Carter in 1980. "I just mind that someone else *is.*"

This explains the rough lack of genuine sympathy in the business, the nasty nervous system of the nation's capital, the almost sexual *shudder* the city enjoys when a major figure takes a fall.

Such a feeling overtook the city when President Bush fired Defense Secretary Donald Rumsfeld right after the Democrats won control of Congress in November 2006. It was the mood that titillated Washington when members of the Senate Judiciary Committee, Republicans as well as Democrats, were pounding away at Attorney General Alberto Gonzales.

I've never forgotten my first exposure to this phenomenon. It was in the summer of 1972 and Richard Nixon was president. At their convention, Democrats had just nominated South Dakota senator George McGovern to run against him. His handpicked ticket mate was Senator Thomas Eagleton of Missouri. Within days, however, the story broke that Eagleton had once been treated for depression with electroshock therapy.

Every professional in the business of politics understood Eagleton was finished. Worse, McGovern knew that whether he kept him on the ticket or asked him to leave, his own thin chances of beating Nixon were now close to none. It wasn't a happy moment for him.

Or me.

Still new to the political world, I asked Senator Frank Moss, my boss at the time, why Tom Eagleton could not be spared. The electroshock treatment episode was in the past. He was okay now. What was the problem?

Unhesitatingly, the senator clued me in. "In this business you take the littlest bitty thing and make it into the biggest thing you ever saw." Think of the roll call of candidates who were forced to learn this lesson the hard way. To name a few: New York governor Nelson Rockefeller's divorce and remarriage just prior to the 1964 election; Michigan governor George Romney's admission in 1967 that he'd been "brainwashed" by generals into an optimistic assessment of the Vietnam War; President Gerald Ford's 1976 debate argument that there was no "Soviet domination of Eastern Europe"; Senator Gary Hart's 1987 relationship with Donna Rice; Senator Bob Kerrey's "lesbian joke" in 1991; Governor Howard Dean's "scream" at an Iowa rally in 2004.

I was still new to Washington during the gory months of Watergate. A presidency, repeatedly struck by scandal, was dying of its wounds. Richard Nixon was clinging to his office even as his senior advisors and top people were dropping like flies. By August 1974, cars were driving past 1600 Pennsylvania Avenue obeying the message displayed on protest posters: "Blow your horn if you want Nixon to resign."

People wallowed in Watergate that summer. Within the White House a president was dead but still walking. A friend of mine working at the World Bank somehow managed to spend his office hours watching the Senate Watergate hearings and his nights regaling me and others with verbal replays—the latest grim dramatis personae of the scandal, meaning Haldeman, Ehrlichman, Colson, and all their lesser henchmen.

In those months, Washington was electric with excitement. An execution was coming. Nobody in a city of power is *ever* late for an execution.

Twenty-four years later, we witnessed a spectacle that resembled it, at least in having that scent of blood in the air. For months, Bill Clinton had denied all, telling television cameras, "I did not have sexual relations with that woman . . . Miss Lewinsky." But the clinical wording he used—"sexual relations"—struck all but the Clinton diehards as a telling indicator of hanky-panky.

By the fall of 1998, President Bill Clinton would be impeached by a partisan House of Representatives, then saved from conviction in the Senate—eviction from the White House—by a less-than-honorable escape hatch. What was provable against him, the affair with the young woman itself, was *not* a crime. The alleged crimes—perjury and obstruction of justice—were not *provable*.

But there had been a period, after the scandal first broke, when the prurient sordidness was close to driving even top Democrats in Congress to demand the chief executive's head. As the president later told friends, he'd been convinced that public anger was so intense that it could have driven him from office.

The sad fact is that Clinton's dishonest denial, "I did not have sexual relations . . ." is what got him past the worst. It was an amoral solution to a problem of immorality.

Whatever you think of the man or his behavior in the matter, Clinton understood key truths about what was happening. He sensed that it was one juncture in his life when "spin" wasn't the answer, when he couldn't charm his way out of trouble. He had to stand there and stonewall, totally and willfully denying the affair to friend and foe alike. Understanding the local culture and knowing how predatory Washington turned when a political hanging was in the offing, he was only too aware that the desire to destroy one person could in an instant become something the entire city might clamor for.

Such awareness makes life tough, I admit. A third of a

century in Washington has shown me the glee people derive from an official's bad fortune. Where the prizes are limited in number—only one person can be president—nothing is both as thrilling and as satisfying as the elimination of a fellow contestant.

As the death rattle of Richard Nixon was sounding, the city could hardly sleep for the sense of festivity. Watergate had been to Washington what Carnival is to Rio de Janeiro. It was Mardi Gras on the Potomac. It had been so much fun, in fact, that when Monicagate hit town, the noisemakers and balloons started to go on sale again.

People like to see that there is one less competitor in the race. Like kids in grade school, they don't mind it at all when someone gets into trouble—as long as it's not them.

Some of the hostility is quite subtle. You may notice in the course of your career certain people becoming cool to you. Try not to take it personally. For whatever reason, they've become your rivals. They either envy what you've got, or they fear you're after what they've got. I felt those unwelcoming responses myself from once-friendly journalists when I switched from political aide to newspaper columnist, and again from TV journalists when I moved from newspapers to television.

It's the world I've chosen. With Hardball and The Chris Matthews Show, I live in the demanding arena of ratings, as well as the rarefied atmosphere of what's known as "buzz." I'm judged by how many people watch me, how many talk about me. If someone is looking at another show, they're not seeing mine. If they tune in to me, they're not watching the other guy. If I succeed, the competition's in trouble.

Bottom Line

Rivalry comes with the territory, if the territory's any good at all. Never be shocked to see that the other fellow—even your best buddy—is rushing to put on his sneakers. Having opposition isn't always comfortable, but it's inevitable.

The only way to avoid this world of zero-sum rivalry is to spend your life seeking what no one else wants.

CHAPTER 13

Nobody Wants
a Level Playing Field

Do what you can, with what you have, where you are.
—TEDDY ROOSEVELT

Sometimes in politics one must duel with skunks
but no one should ever be fool enough
to allow the skunks to choose the weapons.
—SPEAKER OF THE HOUSE JOE CANNON

I WITNESSED SOMETHING POWERFUL at an outdoor campaign rally for Arnold Schwarzenegger during his 2003
run for California governor. Everything about this Modesto
event was purchased: use of the local shopping mall, the
temporary stands, the confetti cannon, the local band. Any
well-funded candidate, Democrat or Republican, running
for any office, could have had it all.

Yet there was a distinct Schwarzenegger difference.

As the Modesto rally was breaking up and the crowd
was leaving, I noticed a young boy, maybe twelve years old,
do something I'd never seen before. He zipped out to the
curb where Schwarzenegger's bus was still parked and, before it pulled away, reached out his hand and touched it.
Having completed his mission, he then went running off,

all the while ignoring the state police who were guarding the area.

It was like watching someone perform a religious devotion. For this boy, it might be the only time in his life he would come that close to global celebrity. Thanks to the magic of the movies, Arnold Schwarzenegger is an icon around the world. That kid wanted to feel, if only for an instant, the power of it all.

Such small spectacles are about the power of dazzle in politics, and also in life. Conventional wisdom has life working in a predictable manner: Insiders most always win; victory goes to those whose turn it is; those in power get to keep it. Then along comes someone who says, "Let's play with a different scorecard." He doesn't spell it out, doesn't have to, but his message clearly is, "I'm here to win this thing."

Suddenly the playing field is no longer level.

Most insiders snickered when Arnold Schwarzenegger, the bodybuilder and action-movie star, said he wanted to be governor of the nation's most populous state. What they failed to see was the fact that he was larger than life already and impossible to ignore.

"Work the difference," another actor-governor of California, Ronald Reagan, once advised. Play to the strengths you have and your rivals lack. It got him elected president.

Harry Reid, now Senate majority leader, played up his experience as a Capitol police officer—the same job that I once had—when he went back home to run for Nevada attorney general. With the District of Columbia's reputation as a high-crime area, the stint put a notch on his belt, suggesting street smarts, and *guts* besides. He'd taken it as a moonlighting job that got him through George Washington University Law School, and later turned it into a campaign plus.

My friend Jerry Rafshoon, an advisor to Jimmy Carter, remembers a night in the Georgia governor's mansion back in 1975. The candidate had a yellow legal pad and was ticking off what he figured should be the selling points of his long-shot run for president:

- Not a lawyer
- Southerner
- Farmer
- Three hundred days to campaign (he was about to end his single term as governor)
- Not part of the Washington scene
- Religious

Rafshoon, who had the job of converting those distinctions into TV ads, worried that many would see those same selling points as shortcomings. "But I think we can make them into assets," Carter said, knowing something nobody else did: that America was so turned off by Watergate—and Ford's pardon of Nixon—that it could elect a *total* outsider.

When the Democrats saw Ronald Reagan coming in the 1960s, they thought they were watching a washed-up movie actor vainly trying for a second career. They dismissed him as the fellow who'd made all those post–World War II B movies, the kind distributed in the late 1940s and early 1950s to provide the second half of a double feature. Even back then, it was clear to me that they didn't know what they were talking about. Ronald Reagan had been a movie star who'd played some powerful roles, such as Notre Dame football hero George Gipp in *Knute Rockne: All American* and the doomed victim of *Kings Row.*

The Dems, however, were blind to Reagan's *true* connection to the American public, that of a television personality. During those Eisenhower years, as host of the highly rated *General Electric Theater,* Reagan had been there in people's living rooms and dens when the politicians were out on what he liked to call "the rubber chicken circuit." I was fully aware of this connection to Americans' fond memories of that era because it was how I knew—and liked—Reagan.

GE Theater fans loved this debonair, credible, comfortable guy. So we paid attention when he entered the political world in 1964, delivering that unforgettable televised campaign speech for Republican presidential candidate Barry Goldwater.

Most Democrats never *got* Reagan, never felt the spell he cast over so many. They somehow lost track of the powerful difference a candidate's TV performance can make. But how could they? Kennedy had been cool and hip, his rival Richard Nixon sweaty and square. Which guy do you think *won* their Great Debate in 1960?

"Work the difference," Reagan would say. If you're good on television, capitalize on that strength. If you're skilled at one-on-one politics, put your faith in that. Reagan was great at the first, notoriously poor at the other. When addressing the country, he had a knack for seeming to be right in the room with us, as if he knew each of us individually. On the other hand, there was often the suspicion that he viewed many around him as interchangeable.

This was the advantage and the disadvantage he came to the table with and he made brilliant use of the first, while paying a grave price—the Iran-Contra scandal—for the second.

In 1991, John Heinz, an active and popular senator from Pennsylvania, was killed in a plane crash. The battle to replace him pitted former governor and U.S. attorney general Richard Thornburgh against Heinz's appointed replacement, Harris Wofford.

Republican Thornburgh began the campaign with a forty-point advantage in the polls. He touted his insider status and connections in TV ads proclaiming that here was a man who "knows the corridors of power."

The soft-spoken Wofford, meanwhile, was running as an outsider. With the economy in recession, he focused on the worries of the average Pennsylvania family—in particular, women's fears that their husbands would be thrown out of work and that they would thus lose their families' medical insurance. "If criminals have a right to a lawyer," he said in a highly effective TV ad, "sick Americans should have the right to see a doctor."

I stopped in at Wofford's headquarters in downtown Philadelphia to find out what his strategists were thinking. Why all the focus on health care? I quizzed consultant Paul Begala. With rampaging unemployment in Pennsylvania, why wasn't Wofford talking about *jobs*?

Begala's answer was masterly.

"*Thornburgh's* for jobs."

In other words, Wofford was taking a position the other side hadn't and, what's more, couldn't. His Republican opponent didn't dare call for "national health insurance" for fear of being ostracized by his own party. Free to claim it as his issue, Harris Wofford could tap into the common gripe that criminals are coddled while the working stiff gets *stiffed*. It was a way for the underdog Democrat to connect with voters' real-life worries.

It was also a compelling example of a campaign knowing not only what it was telling people but what they would be *hearing*. It was one of those "dog whistle" messages in which voters hear something unsaid: It's meant to signal which candidate is looking out for their interests and which one isn't.

Nobody wants a level playing field. The best competitor grabs the high ground and never yields it.

Tip O'Neill well understood the power of the speakership. He knew how much it was about the *appearance* of primacy. Whenever he had to settle a dispute, he invited the warring parties into his East Front office in the Capitol. Closing the doors, he seated himself behind his immense desk—once used by President Grover Cleveland—lit the first cigar, and then never, ever moved from that undeniably singular position.

He had other ploys. When he decreed in a congressman's favor, O'Neill would attack him with such scorn it was almost as if he'd decided the other way. The criticism would temporarily embarrass his beneficiary but at the same time satisfy the one who had, almost without noticing, come out on the short end. People were pleased to see their adversary suffer, and so relieved to escape that over-heated, smoky room that they agreed to accept Tip's judgment and live with his verdict.

All these years later I still recall the thrill of all that cool, clean air entering my lungs after an hour in that hot room inhaling Tip's cigar smoke.

George W. Bush worked the difference when he ran for president. I remember covering his first campaign speech in Portsmouth, New Hampshire, and watching him begin to exploit it. He knew the special advantage he held over the incumbent. He and wife Laura had a calm marriage absent of any public trouble, while Bill Clinton had spent a good part of his second term trying to climb out of the trouble he caused himself and the country after his dalliance with Monica Lewinsky.

Though his rival on the 2000 ballot was actually the clean-living Al Gore, Bush continued to play his difference with Clinton like a virtuoso. With his right hand raised high, he recited at Portsmouth what would be his mantra throughout the campaign. "I think it's important for any of us who assume high office to understand when we put our hand on the Bible that we are swearing not only to uphold the laws of the land—but we are swearing to uphold the dignity of the office to which we have been elected."

For Hillary Clinton, her awareness of her difference in the 2008 presidential race has been on the table from the start. "What is in my background that equips me to deal with bad and evil men?" She was slowly repeating the question an Iowa voter had just asked, and at the same time allowing a knowing smile to cross her face.

Her crowd of boosters loved it. Here was the former First Lady not only slyly conceding that, yes, she had had personal experience of men behaving badly, but she was also glowing with the triumph of surviving it. Moreover, here was a woman who, like so many in that room of supporters, knew the difficulties of staking out your place in a world of men.

Rival Barack Obama began his own quest for the presidency leaning hard on *his* difference: "I recognize there is a certain presumptuousness—a certain audacity—to this announcement," he told an enthralled crowd the day he announced in his home-state capital of Springfield, Illinois.

"I know I haven't spent a lot of time learning the ways of Washington. But I've been there long enough to know that the ways of Washington must change," Obama said.

Listen to former New York mayor Rudolph Giuliani at the 2004 Republican National Convention. Listen to him play up *his* unique selling point: "I don't believe we're right about everything and the Democrats are wrong about everything. Neither party has a monopoly on virtue. But I do believe that there are times in our history when our ideas are more necessary and important for what we are facing. There are times when leadership is the most important."

Rudy's message was a coded one. What he was saying, really, was, Okay, so I'm pro-choice on abortion. Okay, I believe in gun control, especially in big cities. But I was the right leader in a dangerous place when my city needed me—September 11, 2001, and its painful aftermath—and I'm ready to be that kind of unifying leader again.

Bottom Line

Politicians teach us the crucial need to win the war with the weapons we have. Never forget the line from the old Walt Disney movie *So Dear to My Heart*: "It's not what you got. It's what you do with what you got that counts." Especially if the other guy doesn't got it!

CHAPTER 14

Fire When Ready

> *When angry, count ten before you speak;*
> *if very angry, count to one hundred.*
> —THOMAS JEFFERSON

> *I've been right and I've been paranoid*
> *and it's better being paranoid.*
> —WILLIAM SAFIRE

SENATOR GEORGE ALLEN of Virginia started 2006 as a bright prospect for the 2008 Republican presidential nomination. A tall, witty guy, he is the son and namesake of a famous NFL football coach. I had picked him as the Republican with a chance to unite the evangelical and secular wings of his party. Yet one August day out on the road, campaigning for reelection to the Senate, he lost his temper and his political future simultaneously.

What triggered his fateful outburst was the doggedness of one of his Democratic rival's campaign volunteers. S. R. Sidarth, a young man of Indian descent, had been videotaping Allen's campaign stops. Finally, at one rally, Allen decided to point out to the crowd the interloper in their midst.

"This fellow here," Allen said, "over here with the yellow shirt, Macaca, or whatever his name is. He's with my opponent. He's following us around everywhere. And it's just great. Let's give a welcome to Macaca here. Welcome to America and the real world of Virginia."

Macaca refers to a genus of monkey, and is a racial slur used in parts of North Africa, where Allen's mother had grown up.

From that moment until Election Day, the Virginia U.S. Senate race would be about only those few seconds of video. His impulsive words—"Macaca, or whatever his name is"—became a top hit on YouTube. Those ten seconds doomed Allen. Before they occurred, he was a guy on the express train to the presidency; afterward, he was on a side rail back to his law practice.

I've discussed rivalry, about how it comes with the territory, especially for the ambitious, how it can be brutally zero-sum, how it's necessary to find your advantage and use it. Yet all your hard work can be undone in a nanosecond.

The time has come, therefore, to talk about the *ten-second rule.* It's a trick I picked up as I made my way from the scrappy local politics of Philadelphia to the presidential wars of Washington. No matter how great the temptation to spit out a snappy response or clever thought, *count to ten* before you do. This is especially true if you're angry.

How do I know this? Because I've seen that the professionals with the most savvy, the ones who survive and prevail, do it. Give them the opening, offer a sly, negative aside about a mutual acquaintance, and they'll look you in the eye—you can almost see them counting—only to respond noncommittally with something along the lines of: "I'm surprised to hear you say that" or "That's interesting."

The beauty of such an exchange is that *you* have just given away something of value: the fact that you don't like someone. Your friend, the politician, now knows something about you he didn't know before. In return, he's handed you nothing you can ever use.

This is very revealing of political life. It shows how naturally *calculating* the professionals and the natural politicos are. They know, and therefore can teach *us,* that few things are as dangerous as impulse. Nothing is more reckless than an off-the-cuff reply or more durable than its aftermath. The history of American politics is littered with the horrid headlines on those candidates who broke Jefferson's count-to-ten rule.

For example, in the fall of 1948, New York governor Thomas Dewey was winding up his campaign for president against incumbent Harry Truman, whom he was favored to beat. As he whistle-stopped in a small Illinois town, the train from which he was speaking suddenly lurched backward. Though there were no injuries, the Republican candidate made the mistake of allowing his pique to show.

"That's the first idiot I've had for an engineer," he explained testily. "He probably ought to be shot at sunrise, but I suppose we can let him off because no one was hurt."

Dewey undoubtedly was thrown off his stride by the disruption, but, unfortunately, he had forgotten to count to ten! The throwaway remark, with its contemptuous tone, was instantly taken up by the labor unions and used to convince the rank and file that here was a man who naturally would never have their best interests at heart. The comment may well have played a small part in Dewey's surprise defeat at the polls a few weeks later, which allowed Truman to hold on to his job.

In 1966, President Lyndon Johnson became upset when former vice president Richard Nixon called his talk of a mutual withdrawal of military forces from South Vietnam by the Americans and the North Vietnamese an American "surrender" of its military advantage in that country. Johnson caught Nixon's remarks on the way to a press conference and the word *surrender* had stuck in his craw. It was the Friday before the midterm congressional elections and LBJ figured he would take an easy shot at a figure he considered a political has-been. Before the national press corps and TV cameras, he contemptuously dismissed Nixon as a "chronic campaigner."

In that unconsidered instant, Johnson transformed Nixon into the Republican Party's top standard-bearer. Two nights later, the GOP bought thirty minutes of national television time for Nixon to respond to the Democratic president. He made good use of it.

First, he made sure to characterize the Johnson comment as "one of the most savage personal assaults ever leveled by a president." He then pretended to soften the blow: "I understand how a man can be very, very tired and how his temper then can be very short." But genuine sympathy from Richard Nixon wasn't the idea, and his fellow Republicans got it. The GOP made huge gains in the election, and Nixon received the bulk of the credit. He went on to win the Republican nomination in 1968, succeeding Johnson in office.

. . .

In his 1976 vice presidential debate with Walter Mondale, Kansas senator Bob Dole became angered by relentless Democratic attacks on the Vietnam War. He decided to blame World War I, World War II, and Vietnam on the party in power when those wars began. "I figured it out the other day. If you added up the killed and wounded in Democrat wars in this century, it would be about 1.6 million Americans—enough to fill the city of Detroit."

That "Democrat wars" remark hurt Dole badly. It painted a man who was a heroic disabled World War II vet as a poster boy for nastiness. Later, the witty Kansan sought to take the edge off the comment. He said he had been given the partisan job of going after the Carter-Mondale ticket and overdid it. "They told me to go for the jugular," he said. "So I did—mine."

In 1988, the elder George Bush surprised the country by selecting Dan Quayle, an untested, often overlooked Indiana senator as his vice presidential running mate. Years later, Bush would note in his diary that the selection was a mistake.

But Quayle had taken to the campaign trail with wild enthusiasm. From time to time he would compare his record of service in the House and Senate to that of the canonized John F. Kennedy. His staff had warned him of the dangers: Nobody, least of all a politically slight Hoosier, should dare make such a vainglorious comparison.

Yet when it mattered most, in his nationally televised debate with Texas senator Lloyd Bentsen, the Democratic vice presidential nominee, Quayle forgot the strict admonition to keep JFK out of it. Challenged about his youth and undistinguished record, he couldn't contain himself: "I have as much experience in the Congress as Jack Kennedy did when he sought the presidency."

Sniffing victory, Bentsen turned on his young rival like a battleship positioning its big guns on a small, slow-moving freighter.

"I served with Jack Kennedy." Bang!

"I knew Jack Kennedy." Bang!

"Jack Kennedy was a friend of mine." Bang!

Then, the full cannonade.

"Senator, you're no Jack Kennedy."

The stricken look on Quayle's face said it all.

I've already talked about Bill Clinton's failed foray into student politics at Georgetown University, how despite his big-man-on-campus reputation—or possibly because of it—he lost the race for student-body president in his junior year. Yet even back then, the future Arkansas politico was showing his moxie. Whenever his pals tried to get him to say something about his rival in that race, Clinton couldn't be budged.

"Bill would never say, 'That guy's an asshole,'" biographer David Maraniss quotes one of his classmates as saying. "He would say, 'That's an interesting guy' or whatever. We used to kid him about that. 'Come on Bill,' we'd say . . . but his basic instinct was to find, even in the most obvious asshole, something good. We wanted him to get angry in that campaign but he would not do it."

Student politics can get extremely personal. It's all too easy to say something about a rival that you'll regret for the rest of your life. On that score, wise for his years, Bill Clinton knew better.

Bottom Line

Don't react. When you are inclined to take a shot at someone, hold back. Think of Thomas Jefferson, count to ten, and say, "That's interesting." No matter what your field of competition, it does no good to give way to that impulse of yours. It can take ten years to pay for what you say in ten seconds.

CHAPTER 15

Attack from a Defensive Position

The bosses may tell me where to sit. No one tells me where to stand.
—EDWARD MARKEY

There you go again.
—RONALD REAGAN

JOHN McCAIN lost the presidential election of 2008. But he also delivered the wittiest line of the campaign. He said he'd been unable to attend Woodstock, the wild 1969 rock concert, because he was "tied up at the time."

This reference to his capture and imprisonment in North Vietnam conveyed humor, charm, and just the right reminder of personal sacrifice. It was the perfect rebuke to those who found him less hip than his rival.

Edward Markey is the senior congressman from Massachusetts and the dean of the New England congressional delegation. He is the chairman of the House Subcommittee on Telecommunications and the Internet and also of the newly formed House Select Committee on Energy Independence and Global Warming.

His current stature offers a stark contrast to his humble entry into Congress. Back in 1976, Markey had never even been to Washington. A young member of the Massachusetts legislature, he had gotten himself in trouble with its Democratic leaders by pushing a bill that stopped state judges from keeping up private law practices, a cozy situation that hardly promoted blind justice.

Markey called it a travesty for one judge to try a case before a fellow judge. But the entrenched leaders of the Massachusetts legislature didn't agree. Playing rear guard for the status quo, these pols sought their revenge when the Markey reform bill—backed by Republicans as well as Democrats—passed.

In order to teach him a lesson, they dumped him from his place on the Judiciary Committee, and just to make sure that he got the message, took away his office, forcing him to move his desk into the hallway.

With his enemies attacking, Ed Markey struck back. He announced his candidacy for the U.S. Congress, and shot a television ad showing him standing by his desk out there in the hallway. With his arms crossed, staring straight into the camera, he uttered one of politics' most memorable lines: "The bosses may tell me where to sit. No one tells me where to stand."

Frank Capra couldn't have staged it better. At twenty-nine, Markey defeated eleven opponents in the Democratic primary, overcoming rivals far more seasoned in clubhouse politics. He prevailed because, unlike his back-scratching rivals, he came across to voters not only as reform-minded but as wielding a slingshot to boot. Mr. Markey went to Washington—and he deserved to.

In military terms, it's called the attack from a defensive position. It's how the great Henry V of England won the battle of Agincourt.

With his men starving and wet from their long march from the English Channel, Henry was desperate for battle with the French. Outnumbered four to one, he lacked the forces to commence an attack of his own. His only hope was to lure the enemy into an attack—and into range of his archers—and settle the matter. He did so by moving his army forward and thereby triggering an all-out attack by the French. The strategy worked. The charging, heavily armored French knights became bogged down by the mud; the English bowmen did the rest. Eleven thousand Frenchmen died at Agincourt, and only a hundred of the English.

The principle, which applies to both war and politics, is that the aggressor is never more vulnerable than when he has committed to an attack.

In 1944, Franklin Roosevelt demonstrated one of the greatest-ever deployments of this tactic. The Republicans had accused the president of dispatching a navy destroyer all the way to the farthest reaches of Alaska in order to retrieve his Scottish terrier, Fala, who had accompanied his master there on an inspection tour of American bases. Speaking to the Teamsters union at a black-tie dinner, Roosevelt leveled a killer counterpunch.

"These Republican leaders have not been content with attacks on me, or my wife, or my sons. No, not content with that, they now include my little dog, Fala."

His audience loving it, FDR went for the knockout. "Well, of course, I don't resent attacks, and my family doesn't resent attacks, but Fala does resent them. . . . I am accustomed to hearing falsehoods about myself. . . . But I think I have a right to resent, to object to libelous statements about my dog."

A master at ridicule, he went for the jugular. "You know, Fala is Scotch, and being a Scottie, as soon as he learned that the Republican fiction writers . . . had concocted a story that I had left him behind on the Aleutian Islands and had sent a destroyer back to find him—at a cost to the taxpayers of two or three or eight or twenty million dollars—his Scotch soul was furious. He has not been the same dog since."

Once again, the attack from the defensive position.

Four years later, President Harry Truman, who had taken office upon Roosevelt's death, pulled off a similar triumph. He did it in the heat of the battle, when the July 1948 temperature was still ninety-plus degrees in Philadelphia at a late-night session of the Democratic National Convention.

Aware that his party would be facing a brutal onslaught by the Republicans that year, he used his speech accepting the presidential nomination to call the Republican-controlled Congress, which had adjourned for the election, back into session. His diabolically straightforward strategy was to demand that the heavily favored Republicans spend the next several weeks passing legislation to fulfill all the high-flying campaign promises they had been making.

Suffering from miserable poll numbers, and predicted to lose the election, Truman thereby instantly converted the Republican demand for change into a reelection asset.

He turned his opponents' best case against them. They claimed they wanted the Democratic president out of office so they could make good on their promises—and here was Truman telling the Republican-dominated Congress: Go ahead, do what you said you were going to do. Don't let me get in your way.

The 1980 presidential debate between Ronald Reagan and President Jimmy Carter featured another classic attack from a defensive position. The incumbent went after the challenger with everything he had. At one point, Carter threw a roundhouse punch. He accused Reagan of beginning his political career in the early 1960s as a pitchman against Medicare, the popular system of health insurance for retirees.

"There you go again," Reagan replied cheerfully, not seeming to mind the attack, and the audience couldn't help but titter. He had tagged Carter with a well-practiced uppercut. He simply took the president's shot, made it look cheap and worn-out, and slugged it right back at him.

Rather than reply in anger, which would have given Carter's short shot some punch, Reagan seemed to be saying, "Is that the best you can do? To go back and trash something I supposedly said a *generation* ago?" Suddenly Jimmy Carter, who had once run for the presidency as a fresh, sun-in-his-face outsider, looked like another indoor hack pathetically clinging to office.

Reagan's strategy against Jimmy Carter was to refuse to stand still and submit to the incumbent's tiresome efforts to assign blame. Reagan would win reelection in 1984 by executing against another Dem the same maneuver he had used in the debate with Carter in 1980. In their first prime-time encounter, that fall, his opponent, Walter Mondale, had prevailed. "Is the Oldest U.S. President Now Showing His Age?" *The Wall Street Journal* bluntly wondered from the top of its front page.

For the rematch, smartly armed by his TV consultant Roger Ailes, the seventy-three-year-old Reagan was ready. When a reporter asked him in the second debate if he had the "high energy and quick judgment" so crucial in a crisis, Reagan came out swinging.

His weapon was not a punch, however, but a quip. "I will not make age an issue in this campaign. I am not going to exploit, for political purposes, my opponent's youth and inexperience." Wow.

This refracted bullet hit Mondale exactly where the former vice president felt he had his best and only case to win: the issue of Reagan's advanced years. And when the country saw even Mondale himself unable not to chuckle at the quip, there came a sense that the contest was over.

More recently, the 2006 Missouri race for U.S. Senate offered a similar case of a candidate attacking from a defensive position. Republican Jim Talent was the incumbent, Claire McCaskill the Democratic challenger. After her close victory, I asked McCaskill about the effect of a well-known TV ad that actor Michael J. Fox had done for her. A victim of Parkinson's disease, Fox, purposely without his usual medication, had appeared in a commercial in which he appealed for federal financing of stem cell research.

It wasn't the voters' reaction to the Fox ad that made the decisive impact on her election, she told me. It was, rather, the mimicry of the actor's performance by radio talk show star Rush Limbaugh.

Not content with accusing Michael J. Fox of putting on a show for the cameras, Limbaugh felt the need to demonstrate what he was talking about. Visitors to Rush's website could see the radio star wobbling his body and flailing his arms in wild imitation of the actor.

Limbaugh's display backfired.

McCaskill exploited the attack for all it was worth, raising large amounts of campaign money from those across the country who had caught Limbaugh's over-the-top performance. It was a great case of political jujitsu, using the weight and thrust of your opponent to bring him down.

Bottom Line

The best time to defeat your attacker is at the moment he or she is going after you. It's your best opportunity to blow them out of the saddle. It's also the best time to win the gallery to your side. It's human nature to root for the person under attack and to love seeing the predator take the fall.

CHAPTER 16

Don't Pick on Someone Your Own Size

David is still getting good PR for beating Goliath.
—Lee Atwater

They say you can't do it, but remember,
that doesn't always work.
—Casey Stengel

THE GUTSIEST THING I ever did was drive east across the Verrazano-Narrows Bridge. It was the late winter of 1974, and I had left a hapless congressional campaign I'd been working on in Brooklyn to fight what I hoped would be a winning one of my own in Philadelphia.

With the country immersed in the Watergate scandal, I figured there was at least an outside chance for a reform candidate like myself to beat even an entrenched congressman.

Besides my outsider status, I didn't have much going for me. I hadn't even lived in Philadelphia since I went away to college. No one—except for my younger brother Jim, who would one day embark upon his own political career, and my father, who said, "Maybe people are ready for change"—encouraged this quixotic idea of mine. I knew absolutely no one, certainly not anyone with political clout or a habit of bankrolling politicians.

All I had was a notion that this was the time for me to take on the system. It didn't hurt that I had just spent time as a staffer for Ralph Nader's Capitol Hill News Service. The famed consumer advocate had hired me based on a freelance article on the oil pipeline industry I had published since leaving Senator Moss's office. My Nader ties enhanced my outsider's credibility and further allowed me, in Ronald Reagan's words, to "work the difference."

"4th District Candidate Refuses All Money Gifts," a headline in *The Philadelphia Inquirer* announced on March 17, St. Patrick's Day.

> The Watergate scandal has filtered down to Philadelphia's 4th Congressional District, with one candidate declaring that he will refuse to accept any financial contributions at all. Chris Matthews, a 28-year-old former aide to consumer advocate Ralph Nader, said Friday that he would run a "money-free" campaign for the seat held by Rep. Joshua Eilberg, a Democrat.
>
> Matthews, who filed last week for the May Democratic primary, said he would "neither solicit or accept" financial contributions to his campaign. Instead of television advertising, direct mailings and other traditional campaign tactics, Matthews said he would rely entirely on volunteers to reach voters. Matthews, who was formerly employed as an investigative reporter for Nader's Capitol Hill News Service, blamed the "whole system of private campaign contributions"

for political scandals. "If we have learned anything
from these disclosures," he said, "it is that the small
group of private interests that contribute the bulk
of political campaign finances expect something in
return."

I meant what I was saying.

My cause of clean politics, free of special interest taint,
won an enthusiastic and committed following. I went from
high school to high school, I spoke to one class after another, then asked for supporters. Four hundred young volunteers signed on, joining me for "Honk 'n' Wave" rallies
during the late afternoon rush hour on the district's largest
thoroughfare, Roosevelt Boulevard, and for rallies in shopping malls. I even had a high school band volunteer. My
gung ho student followers delivered 150,000 pieces of
campaign literature door-to-door because a friend back in
D.C. had used a congressman's offset printer to roll off the
"Chris Matthews for Congress" material late at night after
he had finished his own daily workload. Attached to his
first shipment was a note: "You've got steel balls."

Apparently this sentiment was shared by my mentor,
Senator Frank Moss. Although I failed at my outside shot
for a seat in Congress—the incumbent was, in fact, later
indicted on conflict of interest charges and accepted a plea
bargain that required he never seek public office again—
I did rekindle Moss's patronage. I had taken him up on his
suggestion that I "dip a little deeper into these political waters," and he had looked kindly on the effort. And while he
had taken some heat from my opponent, a well-established
Democratic member of Congress who had called to com-

plain that a staffer of his, Rich Sorenson, was up in Philadelphia helping me on weekends, Senator Moss was clearly proud that his former aide had taken his best shot.

That's the way your actions are often measured. By having challenged the all-powerful Philadelphia Democratic machine a third of a century ago, I could be given credit for taking on Goliath.

Don't pick on someone your own size. I remember when my later boss, Tip O'Neill, went head-to-head with President Reagan. It was June 1981, Reagan's first year in office, just weeks after the assassination attempt that had nearly taken his life. The fracas started when O'Neill, the top Democrat in Congress, said Reagan spent too much time listening to wealthy advisors, that he showed "no concern, no regard, no care for the little man in America."

Said O'Neill: "I think that he has very, very selfish people around him, people only of the upper echelon of the wealth of this nation, and they are his advisors. I think he'd do much better if he had brought in some people close to him who are from the working force of America, who have suffered along the line, not those who have made it along the line and forgotten where they've come from."

ABC's Sam Donaldson took the ball and ran with it at the end of a Reagan press conference. "Tip O'Neill says you don't understand about the working people. That you have just a bunch of wealthy and selfish advisors."

Reagan hit back hard. "I know very much about the working people. I grew up in poverty and got what education I got all by myself and so forth, and I think it is sheer demagoguery to pretend that this economic program which we've submitted is not aimed at helping the great cross section of people in this country that have been burdened for too long by big government and high taxes."

It was a good punch. The question for Tip was whether or not to take it lying down. I sat in the room as Tip's seasoned staff argued whether to jab back at the president. I weighed in for counterattack.

After listening to both sides, Tip chose to fight. "I'm going up to the gallery," he told the group. Taking a moment in his private bathroom to comb his hair, he emerged to lead the way to the TV press gallery on the Capitol's third floor. Once there, with cameras crowding him, he said that he, as Speaker of the House, would never accuse a president of the United States of being a "demagogue."

"I assume in the future," O'Neill said, that the president would show "the same respect for the speakership." Then came the roundhouse. "The Reagan program speaks for itself. It is geared to the wealthy."

It wasn't long before there was a call from the White House, suggesting a truce between these two Irish American battlers. The challenger had made his point; the champ had acknowledged it. Now they were a *match*. Tip O'Neill had gone up in class, having taken on a president. By sticking to his liberal beliefs, O'Neill managed to make himself a hero even amid the Reagan Revolution. It was one of those cases where a rivalry enhanced the stature of *both* gentlemen.

Three years later, I'm not happy to say, Tip saw the tables turned. This time he was the big guy with a littler one building a reputation at *his* expense. The new kid aiming his fists was an upstart conservative Republican from Georgia named Newt Gingrich.

A group of new-guard Republicans led by Gingrich had begun using C-SPAN, the cable network that aired congressional debates, as a platform from which to criticize the Democrats' record on national security. Each evening, after the House had finished its business, Gingrich and his merry band went before the cameras and took turns regaling C-SPAN viewers with the other party's record of surrender. With everyone else gone home from the House chamber, what they were really doing was gathering nightly to posture, pretending the Democrats didn't have the stomach to defend themselves, when in fact they had already vacated the premises for the day. It was a wily stunt.

As one Gingrich crony confessed later, "We occasionally made the assertion, 'If anybody disagrees, why don't you come down here and disagree with us?' We would do it rhetorically. We wanted to get the debate on."

Tip O'Neill didn't like what he saw. He decided to pull a trick; he directed that the TV cameras, usually fixed on the member of Congress at the lectern, sweep across the chamber and reveal that it was actually empty.

People watching suddenly realized that Congressman Bob Walker, one of Gingrich's colleagues, was orating to row after row of empty seats. He hurriedly explained the obvious to viewers after being handed an urgent note: "It is my understanding that as I deliver this special order here this evening, the cameras are panning the chamber, demonstrating that there is no one here."

What a moment that was. I still grin just thinking

about it. Lamely, Walker tried repackaging his humiliation as righteous indignation. He called the order for the new camera angle an example of the "arrogance of power." But by then it was too late. The Republicans had been caught playing *Home Alone*.

Nonetheless, the situation escalated. The regular Republican leadership took a stand, siding with the Gingrich upstarts. His temper aggravated, Tip no longer was able to stay cool.

"My personal opinion is this," he said after taking the floor. "You deliberately stood in that well before an empty House and challenged these people, and you challenged their Americanism, and it is the lowest thing that I have ever seen in my thirty-two years in Congress."

The Speaker's charge was judged an ad hominem attack on Newt Gingrich, and thus a violation of the House rules. The battle was on.

Trent Lott, the deputy House leader, successfully called to have O'Neill's words stricken from the record, or, in the language of the House, "taken down." This was the first time such a rebuke had been made to a Speaker of the House since the late eighteenth century.

The flap was Gingrich's career break. It put him on the map. By engaging with the Democrats' top leader, he increased his own stature. He had done to Tip what Tip had done to Reagan: gotten into a fight with someone bigger than himself and with the same good result. Gingrich rode this episode all the way to the Speaker's chair. By challenging Tip O'Neill, he established enough rough equality with the top House leader to be viewed as one himself.

. . .

I cannot forget—nor do I wish to—an episode from my grade school years. It was the time in third grade at St. Christopher's when I took on a fifth-grade bully. Somehow I managed to get behind him and had my arms around the big guy's neck. I found myself holding on for dear life. He couldn't get me off and I was too afraid to let go. It was incredible to realize—as I did in real time—that everyone on the boys' side of the playground was watching, and the confidence it engendered arms me to this day.

Bottom Line

Whatever your arena, take on rivals whose stature can enhance your own. Your audience will applaud the contest and salute the challenge. Given the opportunity, fight "up," not "down." Even if you lose, you'll build up your reputation. Besides, you never know: You might just come out on top.

CHAPTER 17

Rites of Passage

Come you back, you British Soldier,
come you back to Mandalay!
—RUDYARD KIPLING

All men who feel any power of joy in battle know
what it is like when the wolf rises in the heart.
—TEDDY ROOSEVELT

FOR SENATOR JOHN MCCAIN, his moment of testing came on a very specific date: October 26, 1967. It was the day his plane was shot down over Hanoi.

It had been a dangerous mission. He was a navy pilot and his target was a power plant in the center of the North Vietnamese capital. When a surface-to-air missile sheared off his right wing, McCain ejected. Knocked unconscious, both of his arms and one leg broken, he parachuted into a lake. An angry crowd, bitterly weary of the American bombing, dragged him from the water. One Vietnamese broke McCain's shoulder with a rifle butt. He was then thrown into a truck and taken to the notorious Hao Lo Prison, known by the American POWs as the "Hanoi Hilton."

Treatment of the prisoner was brutal. When they saw

McCain being denied medical attention, his fellow American POWs thought he was done for. There were to be five and a half more years of imprisonment and beatings. For two years he was kept in solitary confinement. Still, enduring the torture and loneliness, he grew—absent from his country and suffering for it—to feel an overwhelming patriotism.

The released prisoner of war returned home a different, more serious man than the young hotshot he had been before parachuting out of that A-4 Skyhawk.

He had gone through the fire and come out the other side, in a classic transformation story. Nothing serves a reputation so well as early proof of physical courage. It is something important we like to know about someone right up front, a first chapter that makes a life *story*. We see our protagonist as a person of action, better yet, of good fortune, one who faces a great adventure, stays true to his country and his home, and lives to tell of it.

Theodore Roosevelt is one of the four presidents whose faces are chiseled into Mount Rushmore. Does he deserve to be there with Washington, Jefferson, and Lincoln? You bet. Those who lived in his own era and all who have loved him since think it is only fitting to see him in that majestic setting and company.

He has claims on glory far different, of course, from the other three stone presidents who keep him company there. The Teddy Roosevelt legend is one of rousing high adventure. There is his service in the First U.S. Volunteer Cavalry, otherwise known as the "Rough Riders," the wild bunch he led in the Spanish-American War. A unique company of western cowboys and eastern polo players, the Rough Riders made their mark in such famous skirmishes as Las Guasimas and San Juan Hill. It was Roosevelt who trained this famous outfit and rode out in front of it into battle.

For TR, as he was called, those military encounters in revolutionary Cuba offered a gauntlet that led from youth to manhood. Before his Rough Rider days, Roosevelt had been a sickly child of wealth who spent his youth struggling for his independence. While his career after his triumphant charge up San Juan Hill seems inevitable, it could just as easily have ended with that accomplishment. Yet with the confidence of a proven leader of men and the reputation of a courageous daredevil, he went on to enter our national roster of mythic heroes.

As Winston Churchill once marvelously observed, "There is nothing more exhilarating than to be shot at without result."

Fresh from Sandhurst, the British military academy, he first served on India's northwest frontier. A year after that, young Winston was in the Sudan participating in the last British cavalry charge as a subaltern in the 21st Lancers. Next he returned home, but, after losing a parliamentary race, he took off for South Africa. There, while serving as a war correspondent, he was captured by the Boers, eventually escaping through Portuguese East Africa.

His exploits having won him national attention, young Churchill headed back to England and a brilliant political career. This time his campaign for Parliament was victorious. "Courage," he wrote, "is the greatest of human qualities because it is the quality that guarantees all the others."

It is hard to think of either Teddy Roosevelt or Winston Churchill separate from their early exploits. Those military endeavors in exotic locations helped create their iconic images. Both were heroes long before they were leaders.

The same is true of John F. Kennedy. The first time I heard of the future president was when I saw his World War II exploits featured on the television series *Navy Log*. I learned with the rest of the prime-time audience how his PT boat had been rammed and cut in two by a Japanese destroyer. "It was involuntary," Kennedy quipped when asked how he had become a hero. "They sank my boat."

His modesty aside, Kennedy's actions *after* his boat was struck—how he managed to save the members of his crew—were what made him a true hero. *PT-109* was three miles from shore. To get his men even to relative safety— they were on patrol off the Japanese-held Solomon Islands—Kennedy swam for five hours. He did so with the strap of a badly burnt crewman's life jacket in his teeth. Not content to sit around and risk capture, Kennedy then went out into the waters of the Blackett Strait over and over again, trying to flag down an American ship.

It was this display of youthful guts that launched JFK's political career, just as similar acts of glory had TR's and Churchill's. As Billy Sutton, who was Kennedy's first campaign aide, told me years later, when JFK entered the 1946 race for Congress, World War II clearly was his "best campaign manager." The candidate himself joked about his ambitious father's scheme to "parlay a lost PT boat . . . into a political advantage."

But the young Jack relished it when a proud local booster started the drumbeat that his candidate "had proven himself on foreign soil." And he judged others by the same standard. As his old friend *Washington Post* editor Ben Bradlee told me, Kennedy always spoke of men in terms of their World War II service. For him it was a question of where this or that guy had been during that epic struggle.

Everything Kennedy did, from his sponsorship of the Special Forces, to the creation of the Peace Corps, to the space program, was inspired by his service as a young lieutenant in the South Pacific.

For the greatest of America's twentieth-century presidents, the testing moment came later in life and far from a battlefield. Franklin Delano Roosevelt was stricken with polio at the age of thirty-nine. It changed his life. Like Teddy, his fifth cousin (from a different branch of the patrician Roosevelt clan), he had been born to wealth and social position. This crippling illness, which wrought such sudden devastation, transformed him from a young man of entitlement to a person capable of great empathy, someone who understood pain and recognized it in others.

His achievement in surmounting his affliction, which he managed only through tremendous effort, endowed FDR with a sublime self-confidence that was almost magically infectious. Harry Hopkins said it best: "It seems unreasonable at times but he falls back on something that gives him complete assurance that everything is going to be all right."

As Eleanor Roosevelt put it, "I have never known a man who gave one a greater sense of security." She believed her husband's polio was his "turning point," the ordeal instilling in him a strength and courage he had not had before. He was one of those people, someone observed, with the good luck to grow up slowly.

His personal victory also helped FDR inspire others in facing down the Great Depression. As biographer Jonathan Alter has written, "He had triumphed over hardship and despair and embodies that most motivating of ideas: 'If I can, so can you.'" Because of what FDR had done, he was a beacon to all as evidence that they, too, could get back on their feet. When he pronounced at his first inauguration that "the only thing we have to fear is fear itself," there was an authenticity to those words that made them resonate not just in the ears of his countrymen, but down the halls of history.

Circumstances often make our leaders rise in our estimation. On November 27, 1978, Dianne Feinstein, the president of the San Francisco Board of Supervisors, held a press conference to announce the shocking news that the city's mayor, George Moscone, and a fellow supervisor, Harvey Milk, had been assassinated just minutes before. It was a horrific moment.

Feinstein herself had discovered Milk's body, putting her finger on his wrist to check for a pulse. Now she had been catapulted into the role of the city's chief executive by the fact of hideous crime. "When I became mayor I tried very hard to put the bricks of the city back together again," she once said.

Her composure, her grace under pressure in those days, won her the trust and admiration of San Francisco—which later elected her twice as mayor. It is an important thing to know about this dedicated public servant now serving her fourth term in the U.S. Senate. In a moment that might have caused others to wilt, she stood tall.

When we are aware of such stirring episodes as this in a person's biography, we are often correct to believe—to hope—that he or she may one day do something even greater.

The biographies of leaders who lack a "rite of passage," whose public lives begin and end in politics, lack takeoff. There's a career there, but no story. When the heroic arc you see in the sagas of Teddy and Franklin Roosevelt, of Winston Churchill and John F. Kennedy, is absent, you get only the flat line of ambition.

Bottom Line

Trace it to our primitive roots. Our culture accords special respect to the adult who has been given the opportunity— or has found it—to prove his courage in youth. Whether it is Washington the young officer fighting in the French and Indian War, or Lincoln the "rail-splitter" rising from the log cabin, we want to know where the greatness began. It's why Tom Brokaw's "Greatest Generation," those Americans who fought Hitler then came home to build middle-class America, hold such a revered place in our history.

I am convinced that my two years in southern Africa marked a pivotal juncture for me. Though I didn't escape the Boers like Churchill or rescue my crew in enemy waters like the daring Jack Kennedy, I came back with a thin notch of adventure on my belt.

One person who noticed was my grandmother, who had herself traveled widely in her youth, from Northern Ireland to the new land of America. Grandmom figured out what those years in Swaziland had done for me. Watching my ambitious ascent in Washington, she offered her sharp-eyed appraisal: "It was Africa, wasn't it," knowing with her Orangewoman's toughness that she had *nailed* it.

CHAPTER 18

Keep Good Company

*Associate yourself with men of good quality
if you esteem your own reputation.
For 'tis better to be alone than in bad company.*
—GEORGE WASHINGTON

Birds of a feather flock together.
—GREEK PROVERB

A TRICK I'VE LEARNED FROM POLITICIANS is always to stand to the right when there's a news photographer on the scene. That gets you identified first in the caption, which runs below the photo. Most readers only catch that first name.

Should you end up on the left of the group photo, another useful ploy is to put your arm over the shoulder of the person to your right. Such positioning prevents the photo editor from cropping you out of the picture. Otherwise, that hand of yours rests there unexplained.

Think this advice sounds calculating? In fact, it's even more critical to look around before the picture is snapped. Any politico worth his standing will tell you how much it can matter just whom you're photographed with. Whom you keep company with counts.

I once asked Wayne Owens, who'd given me my start in politics with Senator Moss, for his best career advice. He simply said, "Associate with good people." Wayne got his own start running Bobby Kennedy's 1968 campaign in the western states. He never gave up that Kennedy connection, even though it didn't always win him support in conservative Utah.

Another example of such gilt by association is Pierre Salinger, President Kennedy's press secretary and a prominent figure of the "New Frontier." He somehow managed to evoke in his voice and style the charm of the president he'd served. Through his later career at ABC News—a period when he was based in Paris—the mere mention of Salinger's name made viewers of a certain age think of JFK and that shining era in Washington. While it may have been simply a matter of luck, or being in the right place at the right time, it was a link that continued to enhance his standing.

Politicians know how this works, the far-reaching power of association. Walk into the reception room of any United States senator and your eyes will fall on photos displayed on the walls. World leaders and celebrities will be there to remind you of the importance of the office's main occupant. Such a display is de rigueur.

Joseph Biden was elected to the U.S. Senate at the age of twenty-nine—just old enough to reach the constitutional age of thirty the day he took office. His success followed a campaign one can only applaud for its audacity. For instance, on every doorstep in Delaware his volunteers placed a tabloid-style newspaper that declared on its front page: "Joe Biden Is Creating a Stir in the U.S. Senate and He Isn't Even a Senator Yet."

As Delawareans opened each page of the newspaper, they saw young Biden sitting next to a U.S. senator. The setting was, in every case, an ornate, impressive one of the U.S. Capitol. On the right were policy positions Biden held with regard to the senator's top issue. Those pictures of Biden and company in historic Capitol settings made him look like he'd already been elected. It was a way to enforce the claim that he *belonged* there; after all, he already *was* there.

I know, myself, the magic of success by association. No matter where my career has taken me, people in politics invariably will recall my six years of service with Speaker Tip O'Neill. Whatever benefit has come of this, whatever doors—or hearts—have opened, that's okay by me. Tip is one of the few politicians of modern times to be rated legendary.

Of course it works both ways. Had I been hired by the soon-to-be-disgraced New Jersey congressman back in 1971 for my first Hill job, that would have taken some explaining over the years. For starters, there was the matter of that body that *Life* magazine said had to be removed from his basement.

The skeleton in Barack Obama's closet was the Reverend Jeremiah Wright.

In March 2008, ABC News aired a video of a Wright sermon he gave the Sunday after September 11, 2001, in which he said "America's chickens are coming home to roost." U.S. foreign policy, he angrily declared, was to blame for the attacks on the World Trade Center and the Pentagon. "God damn America," he railed. "God damn America."

To rescue his campaign, Obama first separated himself from Reverend Wright, then delivered his landmark Philadelphia speech on race.

"He knew that Wright's remarks could stir racial fears that could become a cancer on the campaign unless some steps were taken to cut it out, and that he was the only one skillful enough to attempt the operation," *Newsweek* explained.

Famed New York attorney Roy Cohn could never escape one key association. He was chief counsel to Senator Joseph McCarthy in the early 1950s, and lived long past the reckless Communist hunt mounted by his boss. Still, Cohn prophesied that his obituary had already been written. No matter what he did in later life, he said, he would be memorialized in the first paragraph as "chief counsel to Senator Joseph R. McCarthy."

Here's what *The New York Times* wrote on August 3, 1986, when Cohn died:

"Roy M. Cohn, the flamboyant, controversial defense lawyer who was chief counsel to Joseph R. McCarthy's Senate investigations in the 1950s into Communist influence in American life, died yesterday." For three decades, his reputation had remained unsavory, tainted above all by a relationship that had lasted only two years.

Bottom Line

This is a simple lesson but a potent one. Pick your friends and bosses carefully. They are the neon lights that illuminate the way to you, that fairly or unfairly declare your character. Lie with dogs and you'll pick up fleas. Sing in the choir and they'll think you're holy.

CHAPTER 19

Lowball It!

There is no worse mistake in public leadership
than to hold out false hopes soon to be swept away.
—WINSTON CHURCHILL

Nobody takes a beating like a braggart.
—YIDDISH PROVERB

M Y FIRST EXPERIENCE with Nancy Pelosi was brief, delightful, and instructive. The year was 1987. I had just been hired by the *San Francisco Examiner* as Washington bureau chief and she had recently been voted into Congress in a special election.

Will Hearst, the *Examiner*'s publisher, was hosting a lunch to introduce me to the city's political community. He had invited a lively crew of pols and labor types to a favorite hangout, the Washington Square Bar & Grill, known to locals as the "Washbag."

Though I didn't know her at the time, Pelosi made a point of courteously phoning up to say she had a scheduling conflict, that, regretfully, she already had a lunch planned with a group of Chinese American constituents.

She probably wasn't going to be able to make it to the event, but she wanted to wish me well in my new job.

So here's the scene: We're sitting there in the Washbag, me and my new pals, having a terrific lunch with many carafes of white wine and multilayered recountings of the city's colorful political history, when I spot a flash of crimson crossing Washington Square. It's the new congresswoman briskly heading toward us. She was able to personally welcome me to her hometown after all.

At your risk, call it a small point. Such paying attention—to the Chinese luncheon event and Will Hearst's party for me—is a kind of daily choreography, and it's what separates the professional from the amateur, the born player from the wannabe. Nancy Pelosi took good care of both sets of lunch companions on her schedule and everybody was happy. An amateur would have committed to both events, risking offense to both sets of hosts. That would have forced her to either bolt out of the first lunch early or get stuck there and miss the other one. By not committing herself to the second, she kept open the chance of finessing both lunches.

Politicians are wonderfully skilled at being politic with people, understanding how to do good without doing harm. A gentleman, it's been said, is someone who doesn't offend anyone unintentionally. Politicians are usually consummate practioners of the art of making relationships work. Transient those relationships may be, but you go away remembering the encounter when you were the one being focused upon, when you were the one for whom time was made.

But Nancy Pelosi's rise to success is not just about her careful one-on-one handling of people. That first encounter with me showed she also understood the useful principle I call "lowball." It's the art of setting the bar close to the ground so that when you do clear it you look great.

Politicians often employ people to do this for them. It's the political parallel to what General Norman Schwarzkopf calls "shaping the battlefield." Hank Culhane, who worked for the Kennedys, was among the best of advance men. Back in '72, he'd scheduled Senator Ted Kennedy into Salt Lake City to campaign for his former top aide, Wayne Owens. It was my first exposure to the real deal, a well-covered appearance that would dominate the news and give the Owens effort a sizable boost.

Making enough hoopla *happen* was Culhane's job. First he went to the Catholic schools in the Salt Lake area and got the kids released for the day. They were to be out there along the sidewalks cheering for the late president Kennedy's younger brother. He set up the holding room where the candidate would sit until the very last minute, creating incredible anticipation, then a wild burst of excitement when Senator Edward Kennedy and the local hero Wayne Owens marched into the packed hall.

To make sure it seemed packed, Culhane ordered an entire wall of lockers moved, making the room smaller. He wanted people squeezing against one another, creating a palpable air of excitement. Anyone in attendance that day was meant to feel thrilled he'd been lucky enough to get into that room!

But it can work in just the opposite way—especially if

your rival has a hand in it. Back when Richard Nixon was running for the U.S. Senate in 1950, a mole from his opponent's camp offered to advance a Nixon stop at the University of California at Santa Barbara.

All the Nixon people knew was that a volunteer had come forward, offering to set up their candidate with a room full of college students. The possibility of sabotage never occurred to them.

That seemingly helpful operative was the now-legendary dean of campaign dirty tricks, Dick Tuck, a loyalist of Democratic candidate Helen Gahagan Douglas, whose sole mission was to humiliate Nixon. Rather than rent a small room, Tuck instead reserved the most cavernous hall on campus. He sent out flyers trumpeting the arriving Republican candidate's speech on the absolutely scintillating topic of the "International Monetary Fund."

When Richard Nixon turned up, he was all but alone in the vast hall. After offering what the press declared a "disjointed" set of remarks, the angry campaigner vowed: "Dick Tuck, you've made your last advance!" Tuck continued to torment Nixon for years to come.

Finally, Nixon, deciding he needed a Tuck of his own, hired the dirty-tricks-minded staffers whose activities led to Watergate and his downfall.

George W. Bush, as a leader, has neglected to lowball when it might serve him well. He committed a terrible error after American and allied troops had captured Baghdad in the spring of 2003. When the commander in chief stood on that aircraft carrier below the banner "Mission Accomplished," he led his country to believe our task in troubled Iraq was behind us. As we soon discovered, the Iraq War had only just begun.

Bottom Line

In business, it's called exceeding expectations. In professional sports, "beating the spread." Because nothing succeeds like success, nothing is so smart as setting the bar low so you can vault it with style.

CHAPTER 20

When in Doubt, Put It Out

Mr. Corleone is a man who
insists on hearing bad news immediately.
—from the film THE GODFATHER

If it's going to come out eventually,
better have it come out immediately.
—HENRY KISSINGER

IN 2006, VICE PRESIDENT DICK CHENEY accidentally shot a companion in a hunting accident and let the weekend pass without reporting the incident. The victim was a Bush-Cheney campaign contributor. Cheney did not even phone President Bush to explain what had happened.

From *The New York Times,* Tuesday, February 14, 2006:

The White House sought with little success on Monday to quell an uproar over why it took the better part of a day to disclose that Vice President Dick Cheney had accidentally wounded a fellow hunter in Texas on Saturday and why even President Bush initially got an incomplete report on the shooting.

The victim, Harry Whittington, a 78-year-old lawyer, was transferred from the intensive care unit to a private room in a Corpus Christi hospital on Monday. He was listed as stable, with wounds to his face, neck, chest and rib cage from the pellets sprayed at him from 30 yards away by Mr. Cheney's shotgun.

At the White House, Mr. Cheney made no statement on Monday and remained out of public view.

However, the incident itself did not fade from public view, and the Cheney shooting quickly burrowed itself into the public psyche. It became one of the few things everyone knew about the vice president. More than that, it told us something of the attitude he held in his position. He had shot a fellow hunter and, even though it had been an accident, he had tried to keep it quiet.

Instead of owning up publicly to what he had done, Cheney decided to hunker down in the private, privileged world to which he had retreated for the weekend. The message of his silence was stark, blunt, unmistakable: I, Dick Cheney, answer to no one. Very clearly this included the man who had invited him onto the 2000 Republican ticket.

President Bush, too, had violated this when-in-doubt-get-it-out rule a half dozen years earlier. The week before that 2000 election, the story leaked out in Maine that Bush had been arrested up there back in his twenties on a charge of driving under the influence of alcohol.

The story, breaking as it did just days before a presidential election, hurt like hell. The biggest question it raised among professionals was why a politician would keep a story so small-bore as an old DUI charge a secret. Had Bush gotten the anecdote on record almost anytime during his Texas governorship, it would have been just another episode in his history of alcohol recovery. (He had even won credit for having given up drinking.) The old arrest for DUI, and its $150 fine, would have been a one-day fuss. It might even have *added* to his regular-guy image. At a minimum, it would have bolstered his reputation as a fellow who had learned the hard way to dump the habit.

Instead, by keeping the story under wraps, Bush left himself vulnerable to precisely what happened: The DUI story exploding just when it was going to make the most noise.

The best politicians recognize the cost paid for concealment. They understand that, faced with an embarrassment, the shrewd move is to let the story be told. Most important, they know the premium that comes with getting it out *yourself*, while you've still got control of it. Mistakes are human, and screw-ups dog us all. It's simply never that easy to bite the bullet when something's gone wrong and say, as the great New York mayor Fiorella La Guardia once did, *"When I make a mistake, it's a beaut!"*

Soon after taking office, President John F. Kennedy gave the go-ahead to an attempted overthrow of Cuban leader Fidel Castro. A brigade of anti-Castro exiles landed at the Bay of Pigs but was soon routed by the Cuban army. Kennedy quickly took total responsibility for the disaster. The public responded favorably to this time-proven way of demonstrating one's leadership, and JFK's approval numbers rose.

While the man in the street never gets the whole truth, Kennedy understood the value of coming clean and stepping up to the plate.

The natural instinct, the *amateur's* way, is to try to hide a problem. The seasoned politico has learned from experience that when trouble comes, no matter how large or how small, it's (a) not likely to go away on its own and (b) someone has to take the hit for it. Most crucially, it's not a moment to delegate. It will only backfire on you if you try to recruit a stand-in.

What works best is when the top guy himself takes the hit. Better still if he's the one who breaks the story in the first place. It's what Bobby Kennedy liked to call "hanging a lantern on your problem."

An example worth examining is the manner in which George H. W. Bush, the first President Bush, admitted to an unfortunate lack of oratorical ability. I remember sitting in the stands of the Superdome, the site of the 1988 Republican National Convention, as Bush gave his poignant acceptance speech. "I may not be the most eloquent, but I learned early that eloquence won't draw oil from the ground. I may sometimes be awkward, but there's nothing self-conscious in my love of country." It's hard to match such an eloquent admission of ineloquence.

The point is that there is nothing so winning as a person telling the painful truth. As writer Nora Ephron explains it, "When you slip on a banana, people laugh at *you*. But when you tell people you slipped on a banana peel, it's *your* laugh."

Bottom Line

If you've done something wrong, don't sit on it. Tell them fast, because it's the only way to ensure that you're first. Better the sting you invite with an outright confession than the much harder rebuke that too often comes when you let someone else deliver the bad news.

CHAPTER 21

You Only Get One Reputation

*A lie gets halfway around the world before
the truth has a chance to get its pants on.*
—Winston Churchill

*If you don't create a pithy description of yourself,
then the press will do it for you.*
—Al Gore

Early in 2007, Hillary Clinton heard rival Democratic presidential candidate John Edwards level a shot in her direction. The former senator from North Carolina had criticized Democrats in Congress for their "silence" on President Bush's Iraq War policy. Edwards called it a "betrayal" of the lawmakers' political as well as constitutional duties.

Hillary didn't like what she heard, which sounded suspiciously close to a personal swipe at *her*. How could she not see herself as the target? She had been among those voting to authorize the president's 2003 invasion. That being an uncomfortable fact, Hillary had to seize control of the spin. She unleashed her staff on Edwards.

"In 2004, John Edwards used to constantly brag about

running a positive campaign," Clinton spokesman Howard Wolfson said in a statement. "Today, he has unfortunately chosen to operate his campaign with political attacks on Democrats."

Hillary next heard the sound of a Barack Obama backer, Hollywood mogul David Geffen, opening up on her and husband Bill. *New York Times* columnist Maureen Dowd quoted Geffen, a former big-dollar Clinton supporter, calling the ex-president a "reckless guy" who would end up ruining his wife's presidential campaign.

"I don't think anybody believes that in the last six years, all of a sudden Bill Clinton has become a different person," explained Geffen, who was in the process of encouraging deep-pocketed friends to kick in for Obama. He described the Republicans as merely marking time until Hillary had secured the 2008 Democratic nomination, at which point they would pummel her with whatever they had.

Again, Hillary directed her campaign spokesperson to respond quickly. Wolfson didn't mince words, accusing the Obama camp of making "vicious attacks."

Her campaign strategy was now clear. The idea was to attack as out-of-bounds any criticism of Hillary whatsoever, especially any criticism involving Bill Clinton's "personal behavior." She was broadcasting that any such attack would bring on an instant defensive counterattack. The offender would be branded as "bad" himself, meaning someone breaking the most basic rules of decency.

"I think if you're going to get into people's *personal* behavior," Wolfson told me on *Hardball*, "yes, I think that's under the belt."

Why would Hillary show herself to be such an avenging

fury? One answer lies in the fact that the best politicians—the Clintons among them—have found out the hard way a supremely important lesson: *You only get one reputation.* Unless you defend it with all your might, don't expect someone else to.

Bill Clinton and his dedicated team of attack staffers knew this back in 1992. He was running against a man, George H. W. Bush, who had won the presidency by destroying the reputation of an earlier Democratic rival. Through ruthless use of the Willie Horton and "Pledge of Allegiance" issues, he had branded Massachusetts governor Michael Dukakis as a man who would defend neither his wife nor his flag. The Clinton forces were determined not to let history repeat itself, not to be ambushed by Bush forces who had proved they knew how to do it.

More than anyone else, Bill Clinton was aware in 1992 of the areas where he was vulnerable, where his defenses could most easily be penetrated. He and Hillary had even, embarrassingly, been forced to appear on *60 Minutes* right after the Super Bowl in order to quiet questions about their marriage.

To deal with these and other Clinton skeletons, the men and women working for the Democratic candidate constructed a war room in Little Rock. Presided over by aides James Carville and George Stephanopoulos, the staff there had the 24/7 task of shooting down each charge before it could explode.

Stephanopoulos's special value in 1992 was that he had front-line experience. Four years before he had worked for the Dukakis campaign in the race against George Bush. He'd seen firsthand his candidate's big lead demolished by the, Republicans' *nastiness*. He'd watched the GOP operatives led by Lee Atwater translate a seventeen-point Dukakis lead in August into an eight-point Bush victory in November. This had been accomplished by launching a brutal "exposé" of the Democrat's record as Massachusetts governor—with special emphasis on a Dukakis program that allowed weekend furloughs to prisoners serving life sentences without parole.

Later, during a debate, Dukakis had taken a shovel to his own political grave by giving a too-tepid response to a hypothetical question about recidivist criminals: How would he feel if his own wife were raped and murdered by one?

It was a perfect opportunity for the Democrat to show he was human after all. Unfortunately, Mike Dukakis refused to take it, just as he had refused every previous chance to fight fire with fire.

Only in the campaign's final week did the 1988 Democratic candidate realize the edge he had handed away. Five days before Election Day, a high school student in the Philadelphia suburbs asked for political advice. Headed to defeat, Dukakis had an answer ready: "Respond to attacks immediately. Don't let them get away with *anything*."

His failure to do just that became the historical impetus behind the Clintons' strategy. "The purpose of the war room was not just to respond to Republican attacks. It was to respond to them *fast,* even before they were broadcast or published, when the lead of the story was still rolling around in the reporter's mind. Our goal was to ensure that no *unanswered* attack reach the people." This, from George Stephanopoulos, who did his job well.

It's hard to explain why the 1988 lesson of Michael Dukakis's defeat had no such effect on the 2004 presidential campaign of another Massachusetts politician, Senator John Kerry. Are memories so short?

Kerry was hit sharply and powerfully on his Vietnam War service. A group called Swift Boat Veterans for Truth ran a highly effective series of TV ads questioning not just Kerry's opposition to the Vietnam War after returning home but his service *in* the war as well. Watching Vietnam veterans attack him in the commercials, it was hard to tell which they were assaulting—his condemnation of the war in the 1971 Senate hearings or his own combat performance.

Diabolically manipulative, the ads dealt a deadly blow to Kerry's reputation. It was exactly the opposite of what he had clearly hoped would be his *strength* running against Bush, who had done his Vietnam-era service at home in the Texas Air National Guard.

John Kerry had opened his campaign against the younger Bush with a smart salute at the Democratic National Convention and the words, "Reporting for duty." He would end it bearing the scars of those "Swift Boat" ads. The verb *swiftboat* would join the political vocabulary as a term for destroying a rival's reputation.

For Kerry, the irony was awful. He had actually volunteered to serve in the Vietnam War and then bravely faced the fire of the enemy. In the parlance of that war, he had been "in it." Bush had not. Yet it was Kerry who suffered from a steady barrage of sly innuendo against his record and his character.

To this day, John Kerry has never been able to fully explain his failure to counterattack. "They had money behind the lies, and we did not have sufficient money behind the truth." Maybe. We know those putting up the money for the ads were indeed willing to spend millions to ensure a Democratic defeat. The senator also said that it was too difficult to get hold of navy records fast enough to counter the charges.

"We should have put more money behind it," Kerry ruefully confessed later. "They spent something like thirty million dollars, and we didn't. That's just a terrible imbalance when somebody's lying about you." He did contribute to the problem, however, by refusing to authorize a release of his navy service records, a step he eventually took but not until long after the campaign.

The sad truth we learn from all of this is that it's one thing to call your critics "liars," but to regain the political edge you must *prove* they are. Democrats who gave their all to the Kerry campaign came to believe the failure to rebuff the attacks cost him an election for which he and they had worked so hard and which they had come so close to winning.

From watching smart politicians in action, I've learned a few useful ways to protect your reputation. And while nothing prevents someone from attacking your character, these steps can help to protect you before, during, and after the attack.

First: Recognize that attacks on your reputation actually *work*. When something negative's been said about you, people tend to believe it. If you're a stranger to them, they *really* believe it. Voters perpetually tell pollsters how much they just hate the mud that spews forth from campaigns— but it's not the bland, positive ads they remember.

We're often ready to believe the worst. Tell anyone an unseemly or unflattering fact about a person he doesn't know, and it instantly becomes *all* he knows about him. Richard Nixon's first campaign manager, Murray Chotiner, espoused the belief that the average citizen is likely to know just three things about a candidate—and no more.

Keeping that in mind, the best way to win is to design a strategy that gets out three facts or ideas about your opponent, all of them bad. "I say to you in all sincerity that if you do not define the opposition candidate before the election gets started," Chotiner warned his clients, "you are doomed to defeat."

Second: Act quickly!

There's little point in trying to persuade your opponents that a shot that has been taken against you is unfair and untrue. Your number one target for such efforts must be your *friends*. They not only need to hear your side of things, they *want* to hear it. Give them the ammo they need to defend you. And give it to them *fast*. When someone starts heaving the trash at you, you'd better arm your defenders first.

It would have been time wisely spent had John Kerry thought to offer his supporters his own versions of his Vietnam War combat stories before his opponent gave his. As a veteran who had faced death for his country as a U.S. Navy patrol-boat skipper, he owed himself that.

It would have been shrewder still for Kerry to remind the country right up front that he had opposed the war on his return home and, indeed, turned antiwar activist. That way, he would have prepared the voters for the "swiftboating."

Third: When you're in a hole, stop digging!

There may come a time when, all the facts being known, it's simply time to change the subject. Arnold Schwarzenegger was in big trouble early in 2006. He had been elected governor three years earlier on a promise of reform. He had taken office in Terminator mode and mocked his fellow California officeholders as "girly-men" for opposing his measures.

His early disdain came back to hit him in the face when he asked voters to back cost-saving salary cuts for teachers, nurses, and firefighters in a referendum in November 2005. He found that Californians were not as sold on his charms as he had thought.

Because he'd overestimated the mandate given to him by the electorate, Governor Schwarzenegger now stood the risk of losing his 2006 reelection and being discarded as a political amateur who had failed to translate his big-screen popularity into genuine capital. Recognizing political reality, he adjusted his program accordingly. He admitted he had been too "pushy and personal" in attacking the Democratic legislators in Sacramento, and realized it would serve his constituents best if he abandoned his confrontational style for a new model of leadership.

"Instead of Democrats coming up with the policies and Republicans come up with their policies and go and debate over it and compromise, I think it is good to sit down right away, from the beginning *together,* Democrats and Republicans, and talk about the challenges that we face," he announced.

As a result of being able to see the error of his ways, Schwarzenegger won not only a decisive reelection in 2006, but he began 2007 as a major player in national Republican politics, championing a rebirth of the party's moderate wing, which had died during the Reagan and Bush years.

Bottom Line

Construct a war room of your own. When something is said against you, take the initiative in straightening out the record. You only get one reputation. Don't assume that people are not going to believe the worst. As Alice Roosevelt Longworth, who was the daughter of Teddy Roosevelt and the wife of a Speaker of the House, put it, "If you don't have something good to say about someone, come sit next to me."

CHAPTER 22

Aim High

A wise man should ever follow the ways of great men. . . .
He should do as the skillful archer, who,
seeing that the object he desires to hit is too distant . . .
aims higher than the destined mark.
—NICCOLÒ MACHIAVELLI

What makes journalism so fascinating and biography so interesting
is the struggle to answer that simple question:
What's he like?
—JOHN F. KENNEDY

WE ALL HAVE HEROES. Even our heroes have heroes. Jack Kennedy so respected Britain's World War II prime minister, Winston Churchill, that he kept his example continually before him. It was Churchill's notion that the military strength the United States developed in the Cold War was not about *winning* wars but about *avoiding* them. He also believed that World War II might well have been averted had his country and the other democracies been strong in confronting Adolf Hitler earlier. Later, he thought that the Soviet Union could be tempered in its ambitions if faced with a well-armed West, an alliance firm in its resolve.

Churchill believed in a foreign policy two-step: first, arm, then talk. Instead of a conflict with old ally Joseph

Stalin, he wanted a settlement with the Soviet bloc. To get it, the United States and Britain had to arm themselves. "I do not hold that we should rearm in order to fight," he said, after resuming power in 1951. "I hold that we should rearm in order to parlay."

As Kennedy biographer Barbara Leaming has recently documented, this is precisely the policy the young American president backed: exploiting U.S. military prowess for strategic advantage. It's how JFK won his greatest achievement, the limited nuclear test–ban treaty. It also helped him survive his greatest peril, the Cuban Missile Crisis.

In each case, he paid open tribute to the Churchill model: First, build military strength; second, negotiate from that strength. "As Winston Churchill said, 'It is better to jaw-jaw than to war-war,' " JFK liked to say.

President Ronald Reagan looked to that other hero of World War II Franklin Roosevelt as *his* role model. The two American presidents, one a Democratic liberal, the other a Republican conservative, were more similar than you might think. Both men could be coldly impersonal close up, regarding staff and Cabinet members as tools rather than human beings. Yet distance served them well, and both were brilliant at connecting instantly and deeply with the American people at large.

Reagan admitted he had gotten the idea of going over the heads of Democratic lawmakers from FDR's radio "Fireside Chats." He wrote in his memoir how listening to those common-sense broadcasts during the Great Depression, when he himself was a young Iowa radio announcer, had left an "indelible mark" on him. As an actor as well as a politico, President Reagan, who had entered our homes as host of the *General Electric Theater*, was determined to be as effective in the television age as FDR had been in the golden days of radio. Although he rejected the big-government legacy of FDR's New Deal, Reagan never stopped admiring its champion. Just as the aristocratic Roosevelt could speak to the "forgotten man," the movie star–turned–politician could talk in a common language to the midwestern factory worker.

In the late 1930s, when Jerry Paar was a boy, his father had taken him to see an exciting action picture, thrillingly titled *Code of the Secret Service.*

A Secret Service agent in hot pursuit of evil counterfeiters, the film's hero, Brass Bancroft, left such a lasting impression on Paar that he later joined the Secret Service himself. And as the years passed, Paar rose in the ranks to become chief presidential bodyguard. I remember watching him shift from standing behind Jimmy Carter during the inaugural ceremonies on January 20, 1981, to a new position behind Ronald Reagan, once the latter's oath of office had been taken.

Two months later, Paar was guarding Ronald Reagan at that moment when the president walked out the door of the Washington Hilton and a disturbed young man named John Hinckley was waiting to open fire. The first shot hit presidential press secretary James Brady; another wounded D.C. police officer Thomas Delahanty; a third bullet hit Secret Service agent Timothy McCarthy; still another found its target—the president.

Operating on training and instinct—what he called "muscle memory"—Paar took charge of the dramatic situation, shoving Reagan into the back of the presidential limousine, covering him with his body, and yelling, "Let's move!" to the driver.

With his decisive action, Jerry Paar changed history. By shielding Ronald Reagan from further assault by Hinckley, who kept firing as their car sped away, and by getting him to the George Washington University Hospital emergency room in time, he had the honor of saving an American president's life.

Now comes the most fascinating part of the story. The actor who played Brass Bancroft in *Code of the Secret Service,* who inspired Jerry Paar to become an agent himself, was the man Paar saved that day by his courage and quick thinking.

Yes, we all have heroes. Winston Churchill has been my constant role model—for many obvious reasons but, above all, for his readiness, shown early in life, to stand alone. That's something I've tried and had to do through every political debate, not least over the war in Iraq. Keeping the image of the great Churchill before me has made it easier.

When I was in college in the 1960s and thinking about journalism, I hoped to follow in the steps of Joe McGinniss, the Holy Cross grad who became first a columnist for *The Philadelphia Inquirer* and then the author of *The Selling of the President 1968,* a book that forever changed the way we look at presidential politicking.

By the time I arrived in Washington in 1971, as I've said, my goals had shifted and I most admired Theodore Sorensen, the aide who had been John F. Kennedy's speechwriter.

Later in the decade, I became a fan of George F. Will, the columnist and TV commentator. *Hardball* also no doubt owes a debt to William F. Buckley's *Firing Line*. I'd like to think *The Chris Matthews Show* combines the seriousness of the pioneering *Agronsky & Co.* with the fun of *The McLaughlin Group*. Perhaps someday I'll find a distinctive way to match the great Eric Sevareid, whose eloquent commentaries elevated the evening news to *history*.

Bottom Line

It's hard getting somewhere without a map. It's the same reason so many of us love biographies. They show us how others have gotten where we want to go. If you want to get somewhere, study the routes others have taken. As much as I've resisted it at times, there's nothing wrong with stopping to ask directions. Politics has taught me how necessary role models are. Once you have one, or more, you have a personal vision of how you want to spend your life.

CHAPTER 23

Speak Up!

*Of all talents bestowed upon men and women, none is as precious
as the gift of oratory. Abandoned by his party, betrayed by his friends,
stripped of his office, whoever can command this power
is still formidable.*
—WINSTON CHURCHILL

Just imagine that everyone in the audience is naked.
—OLD SHOW BUSINESS ADAGE

I WAS ONCE AFRAID TO GIVE A SPEECH. *Petrified* might be a
better word. I had the deepest fear of standing up and
saying anything in public. I truly dreaded my public-
speaking classes at La Salle College High School back in
Philadelphia, hoping each week that my turn would not
come to stand and deliver. Even as a graduate assistant at
the University of North Carolina at Chapel Hill, I couldn't
sleep on those nights before I was to stand in for the professor.

These days, as you know, I *rush* to the microphone,
whoever the audience, no matter how large. When I sit in
my studio getting ready each night for *Hardball* or preparing each week for *The Chris Matthews Show,* I'm totally at
home.

One experience that got me over the hump was my two-year Peace Corps hitch, when I'd present myself to perfect strangers in Swazi villages. I made further progress when I had to deal with tough reporters in Tip O'Neill's office. I can assure you that the mere act of answering hard questions on the phone, not to mention meeting the high demands placed on me by the Speaker, were confidence-building.

I eventually became self-assured enough to accept just about every invitation to address an audience that came my way. I got so used to standing before a group that I stopped worrying about it. In fact, I was having fun, especially with the chance to poke at the absurdity of certain political posturings.

It has been hardest for me, interestingly enough, to get completely comfortable doing *The Tonight Show*. Part of it is the band, which sets a high standard for performance. The other factor is the studio audience that sits out there waiting to be entertained.

When I stand backstage waiting to be introduced, I carefully rehearse in my head the big right angle I'll take on the stage to shake hands with Jay Leno, the big "Miss America Wave" my producer Tammy Haddad has taught me, my right arm bent high over my head. Someday even this will be natural. Practice, I've learned, makes *anything* perfect.

The irony is that I was *writing* speeches years before I was any good at speaking publicly myself. It started right after I got back from the Peace Corps, back when I had that job as a U.S. Capitol policeman. I'd sit at my desk in the Capitol basement, guarding a tunnel with my .38 Police Special.

Stuffed in the drawer would be the latest draft of a speech I was writing for Senator Moss.

It was far more thrilling, eight years later, when I found myself on Air Force One typing President Carter's speeches. It wasn't until I was working for Tip O'Neill, day after exciting day, that I learned to turn out snappy political one-liners on demand.

Along the way, I learned a few things. One trick I've developed is outlining a speech with just a few words to cue me. This has become easier and easier as I've been able to build up a reliable reservoir of material. Only recently have I learned to *write* my speeches ahead of time as if I were preparing them for one of my old bosses. The big occasion—especially college and university commencement addresses—demands that you get all the words right well in advance.

A speech should be no less than ten minutes, no more than twenty. The very best—Lincoln's Second Inaugural, Martin Luther King, Jr.'s "I Have a Dream," Kennedy's Inaugural—were solidly constructed and to the point. And of course the Gettysburg Address was incredibly brief, hardly more than a minute when I read it aloud.

So here goes! A good speech has six parts:

1. *The icebreaker:* First, offer a quip about the occasion. This is to relax the crowd and stamp the moment with your voice and personality. It can be hokey—"At least you can't blame me for this weather"—or it can be an all-occasion greeting: "As King Henry VIII said to each of his seven wives, 'I won't keep you long.'" The goal is to simply let the audience know you're there for *them*.

2. *The tease:* Next, give a provocative glimpse of what your speech will be about. This is important. Like a stripper letting loose of the first shoulder strap, your goal is to rivet the audience's attention to what you're about to pull off. "What I am about to tell you will shock you" isn't bad.

3. *Anecdote time!* Be prepared with a few appealing stories about the specific place, person, or occasion that has brought you there. The idea is to further connect with your listeners. Consider this your final warm-up before takeoff. Try to find the anecdotes that will spotlight a few individuals in the crowd sitting in front of you. It instantly converts an audience into a community.

4. *Download:* Okay, tell them what you've traveled there to say. Just hit it—point by point.

5. *Relief!* Time to let them know the heaviest part of the speech is behind them. Just tell some light-hearted story that brings your message home.

6. *Send-off:* Go for high octane! You want to leave your audience with a "wow." Think of the reason you came to speak, then belt it for all to hear. If nothing else, it will alert everyone that you're done and it's time to clap.

Bottom Line

Being able to express yourself, to make your ideas not just listened to but *heard,* is important in just about every situation, from corporate meetings to family conclaves. Nothing makes a job like this easier—and less daunting—than to break it up into tasks. It's like dividing the enemy before a battle. Just look at each of the six steps and fill in the blanks: icebreaker, tease, anecdote, download, relief, and *send-off*. And don't worry. This six-step system is a wonder. It works for me; it will work for you.

CHAPTER 24

The Bug

I run for president because that's where the action is.
—JOHN F. KENNEDY

It's easier to run for president than to stop.
—EUGENE McCARTHY,
PRESIDENTIAL CANDIDATE '68, '72, '76, '88, '92

WHAT MAKES THE BEST POLITICIANS different from other people is something akin to a chronic condition. It's the bug from which none want to be cured. It's what bit them, what drives them on to crave higher and higher office. It's always the "next" that matters above all.

Bob Casey, a man steeped in Pennsylvania politics and who served two terms as governor, is a good case study. I know because his is my home state, too, and I observed him for a couple of decades. When he was elected a Democratic state senator from Scranton in 1962, he decided right then and there that his next job was inevitable: He was going to be the state's next chief executive.

Years later he would look back at his chutzpah and shake his head in disbelief: "I was thirty-four, knew everything, and felt just sure I was ready to run the whole show. I marvel at my audacity at the time. But some young men are like that, and I was the most self-assured of the type."

Not everyone shared his vision of his political future. Pennsylvania's elder statesman former governor David Lawrence told the brash legislator to his face to forget it. "Your candidacy makes no sense. You're too young. You're not identified with any statewide issue and, besides, you're Catholic." A few years earlier, Lawrence, himself a Catholic, had been publicly skeptical that *Jack Kennedy* could carry the state.

Casey ran anyway and found himself beaten in the gubernatorial primary by a cable television millionaire, Milton Shapp, a fellow perfectly willing to spend as much money as needed to convince the voters to pull the lever for him.

Four years later, Bob Casey was right back at it again. Once more his rival for the Democratic nomination was Shapp, and again Casey appealed to old-line big shots for their support. In this case, the go-to guy in the state was Philadelphia mayor James H. J. Tate. Tate decided to endorse Casey in the classic fashion of the old political boss. "I am supporting Casey as long as he behaves himself," he said. But Casey hated looking like Tate's stooge and went public with the fact. "If I win this election," he declared, "I'm going to be the governor of Pennsylvania and nobody else. If Mayor Tate has any different view, he'd better rethink his position." That was the end of the Philadelphia mayor's endorsement.

In 1978, Casey tried for the *third* time to gain the Pennsylvania executive mansion. This time he was the victim of the fact that there was suddenly a confusing number of statewide office-seekers named "Robert Casey." One had already gotten elected state treasurer. Now another Robert Casey was seeking the Democratic nomination for lieutenant governor on the same ballot as the determined young man who'd spent years building the brand.

The presence on the ballot of an identically named contender may not have been the reason he lost his race again, but it sure couldn't have helped. People had reason to believe they could nominate Pittsburgh mayor Pete Flaherty for governor and Bob Casey for *lieutenant* governor. The genuine article—the Robert Casey with the bug in his gut for the gubernatorial slot—was once again the also-ran. As one commentator dryly observed, "Casey's name is magic for everyone *but* him."

Eight years later, in 1986, the Bob Casey who'd been eyeing the governor's job from the moment he first entered the state legislature was ready to try yet again for the prize. "I had no campaign staff in waiting," he wrote later. "No financiers eager to bankroll my *fourth* run for governor. No pundits calling on me to return to politics for the good of the state. For all practical purposes, I had nobody and nothing." He also faced the prospect of running against the mayors of Philadelphia and Pittsburgh for the nomination.

But at last Casey's single-minded pursuit landed him in the right place at the right time. Dubbed "the three-time loss from Holy Cross" (yes, my alma mater), the man harboring that ferocious bug to be governor had reached the goal he'd made his dream twenty years before. And when he was reelected after serving his first term, he won by over a million votes, the biggest landslide in Pennsylvania history.

• • •

There is nothing partisan about the bug. Republican Arlen Specter was elected district attorney of Philadelphia in 1965. Two years later he ran for mayor, a long shot for a GOP candidate in the deeply Democratic city, and lost. Six years later he was defeated for reelection as D.A. But what might have cashed out other political careers didn't stop Specter.

Escalating his ambitions if not his chances, he ran a good race for the Republican nomination for U.S. senator and lost. That was in 1976. Two years after that he ran for Pennsylvania governor and lost. In 1980 he ran for the U.S. Senate and won, then went on to gain four more terms. He had pursued office for fifteen years with largely unsuccessful results, followed by a thirty-year record of uninterrupted and satisfying public service.

Winston Churchill, arguably the most courageous democratic figure in history, caught the bug at a young age. In 1899, at the age of twenty-five, he launched himself into the political arena. He had resigned his commission in the British Army and was standing for Parliament as a Conservative candidate. Here's a snapshot of his early political life, as described to his then-girlfriend Pamela Plowden:

> It has been a strange experience and I shall never forget the succession of great halls packed with excited people until there was no room for a single person more, speech after speech, meeting after meeting— three, even four in one night—intermittent flashes of heat and light and enthusiasm with cold air and the

rattle of the carriage in between: a great experience
and I improve every time. I have hardly repeated myself at all.

Read between the lines—and if you're like me, it's almost as good as being there. Can't you just feel his happiness, his joy in the sport of it, the thrill he felt with
constituents cramming in to see him, the heady sensations
brought on by the experience of his words swaying eager
listeners? Every politician worth the name knows the feeling.

Churchill lost that first race for Parliament. After winning a seat following his celebrated escape from the Boers
in 1900, he lost again in 1908 when he first sought reelection as a member of the new Liberal government. He lost
three times in the 1920s and again in 1945 despite the fact
that he, as Britain's prime minister, had led the victorious
fight against Adolf Hitler. Undaunted, he led his party back
to power six years later.

His ally Anthony Eden described Churchill's long and
indefatigable public life: "Courage for some sudden act,
maybe in the heat of battle, we all respect, but there is that
still rarer courage which can sustain repeated disappointment, unexpected failure, and shattering defeat. Churchill
had that too and bad need of it, not for a day, but for weeks
and months and years."

Abraham Lincoln, in the almost century and a half since
his assassination, has become this country's most mythic
figure, our universally agreed-upon secular saint. Yet he,
too, undeniably had the bug, and even he suffered setbacks

along the way to the presidency. In 1832, he was defeated for the Illinois legislature in his first race; in 1846, he was elected to the U.S. House of Representatives for a single term; in 1855 he ran for the U.S. Senate and lost; in 1858 he ran again for the Senate, winning the popular vote over Stephen Douglas but losing the victory when his candidacy was shot down in the Illinois legislature, as was then legal; in 1860, he was elected president and went on to become our country's most revered leader.

Bottom Line

Ambition won't guarantee victory—but few triumph without it. What I've learned from politicians is how trying, then trying again, can change a loser into a winner—and that victory rarely comes on the first attempt.

CHAPTER 25

Wherever You Go, That's Where You're Going to Be

Think of these things: whence you came, where you are going, and to whom you must account.
—Benjamin Franklin

Let us endeavor to live that when we come to die even the undertaker will be sorry.
—Mark Twain

I REMEMBER TWO BITS OF ADVICE Senator Edmund Muskie gave those of us on his staff the night he won his last Senate election from Maine. The victory party was at the Monocle, a restaurant and bar near the Senate buildings. Muskie had downed a number of strong martinis, we figured, and was of a philosophical bent. That was lucky for us because I've remembered the two things he said that night with impressive force.

The first was a motto he credited to Clark Clifford, the Washington superlawyer who famously helped mastermind Harry Truman's upset of 1948. "Wherever you go," he quoted Clifford as saying, "that's where you're going to be."

At the time I took it to mean that Muskie was telling

his staffers to think hard about where their ambitions might take them. A Democrat, Jimmy Carter, had just been elected president, and Muskie may have been thinking about his own future. Within three years, he would be secretary of state. Myself, I took it very much to heart. Why get into a lather about this or that job if I wasn't sure it was where I wanted to end up? It's not the direction you set, he was warning us younger folk. It is the destination that awaits you.

That could be good advice for the reader of this book. I've spent all these chapters instructing you on the *how* and the *how-to,* not the *what* and the *why.* Yet it is the possession of a clear purpose that sets apart the great politicians from the lesser. I remember a very sage pollster, a Canadian named Allen Gregg, explaining how every great leader possesses three key attributes: motive, passion, and spontaneity.

We certainly can't think of any of our great U.S. leaders separately from their historic missions: Lincoln to end the expansion of slavery and to save the union, Roosevelt to rescue the "forgotten man" from the Great Depression and lead the country to victory in World War II, Kennedy to protect mankind from nuclear war, Reagan to expand and protect freedom by defeating Soviet communism and limiting big government.

Think of Al Gore as a presidential candidate in 2000 and later as an advocate for public awareness of global climate change. The Gore of 2000, though a politician for much of his adulthood, lacked a clear motive for his public life. He spent much of that year's presidential campaign talking relentlessly about a "lock box" to protect payroll taxes for use in Social Security benefits. It would prove less effective as a campaign promise than as satirical material for *Saturday Night Live*.

Yet when Gore returned to the public stage in 2006 as an informed crusader for global warming, he now took on the mantle of a widely *respected* world figure. Why? Because this time he had a reason for being in public life.

This brings me to the second bit of advice Senator Muskie shared with the troops that misty night in November 1976. Having just won a hard race for reelection in a state where being a Democrat was an obstacle to overcome, he was feeling the power that comes with having once again bucked the odds. "The only reason to be in politics," he told us, "is to be out there all alone and then be proven right."

This is what gives the special edge to the person with a worthy motive in life: the willingness to take up a cause that is not currently popular. It's why I like to ask any group of young people I meet if there's anyone in the room who holds a view on a public matter that they know to be unpopular with the group. I tell those who volunteer with genuine, heartfelt *minority* positions that they are tomorrow's future. I want that so much to be true for the very personal reason that I've devoted my life, it seems, to relentlessly championing views that were the very opposite of prevailing wisdom. While I can't say that I've always enjoyed being out there all alone, I have relished the challenge of doing just that.

Bottom Line

Find a mission in this world that's worthy of all your work, your wit, your life. It's what I would say to anyone making a potentially momentous personal decision, the same thing I'd tell someone deciding to run for elected office: Stay up late one night, and well past midnight, when you're all alone, ask yourself, "Why am I doing this thing?" There's no wrong answer, no right one. But it sure helps clear things up to know what that answer *is*. This book is packed with well-practiced *hows*. Your very personal mission is to supply the *whys*.

Acknowledgments

Ernest Hemingway wrote "There are some things which cannot be learned quickly, and time, which is all we have, must be paid heavily for their acquiring." Each discovery presented in this book resulted from real-life experience in the rival worlds of politics and journalism.

It was during that powerful half dozen years with Thomas P. "Tip" O'Neill, Jr., that I began paying serious attention to political tradecraft. It was Kirk O'Donnell, the Speaker's chief counsel, who prompted me to see that politics is not helter-skelter, that there are certain codes to the business, O'Neill himself having been their great practitioner.

I owe my political education on the whole to the long march of people who have entrusted me to join their inner circles. The chapter title "It's Not Crowded at the Top" is entirely the truth. Even my entry job as a Capitol policeman was a prize for someone arriving in Washington without connections, as I did. Certainly the chances that came later—to serve the U.S. Senate, the White House, and a legendary Speaker—are rare, and even more rarely do they arrive in a single career.

So the first of those I need to thank for *The Hardball Handbook* are the people I've showcased in the book whose stories and examples are the key to everything I've learned and shared with you: Wayne Owens; Senator Frank Moss; Mary Jane Dew, the AA who brought me back to Moss's office in 1974; Ralph Nader, who personally picked me for his Capitol Hill News Service; Bob Schiffer, who became my lifelong friend in a congressional campaign in Brooklyn and then helped me in my own campaign in Philadelphia; Rich Sorenson, who inherited my job with Frank Moss and devoted many a weekend cheering and helping me in that same hopeful primary race in '74.

I want to thank, more than I have before, the impressive Richard Pettigrew, who brought me to the White House as one of his deputies in the President's Reorganization Project, and Hendrik Hertzberg, President Carter's chief speechwriter, for making me one of his colleagues.

For my second career, writing for newspapers and working on television—the latter now having well exceeded the first in years—I owe Larry Kramer, who made the big decision to make me Washington bureau chief for the *San Francisco Examiner*. For their great support and friendship there and later, when we all moved to the *Chronicle*, I thank publisher Will Hearst, Gail Bensinger, Phil Bronstein, Jim Fine-frock, Paul Wilner, Kandace Bender, and so many others.

For bringing me to television, I owe Sir Howard Stringer, David Corvo, and Jack Riley. For giving me a show of my own, I must thank Roger Ailes. For *The Chris Matthews Show* I thank former NBC News president Neal Shapiro and the folks at NBC Universal syndication. For backing me up at MSNBC and NBC all these years, I most need to thank MSNBC president Phil Griffin, NBC News president Steve Capus, former NBC chairman Bob Wright and his wife, Suzanne, and NBC chairman Jeff Zucker.

For *Hardball,* I thank executive producer John Reiss, Tammy Haddad, Tina Urbanski, Jeremy Bronson, Brooke Brower, Colleen King, Ann Klenk, Connie Patsalos, Shelby Poduch, Querry Robinson, Stephen Samaniego, Beck Schoenfeld, David Shuster, Vidhya Murugesan, Roland Woerner, Moshe Arenstein, Court Harson, Ray Herbert, Rick Jefferson, Lauren Moore, Chris Pendy, Robbi Blevins, Derbin Cabell, Drew Fredrickson, Nikki Iannucci, Gary Lynn, Alicia Majeed, George Toman, and Carl Trost.

For *The Chris Matthews Show,* I owe much to Nancy Nathan, my executive producer, Reihan Salam, Bill Hat-field, Michael Levine, Jeffrey Blount, Bantu Opiotennione, Demetrea Triantafillides, Regina Blackburn, Gina Wilson, Ron Thornton, Mike Benetato, Susan Vitorovich, Keith Gaskin, Marsha Groome, Dave Hanson, Steve Mitnick, Jim Hughes, Pat Kehs, Chris Williamson, Mario Racine, Jackie Thompson, Mike Higgins, Ed Wallace, Dave Lurch, Scott Fowler, Mary Manby, Colleen Clapp, Katherine Zwicky, Jay

Stein, Bobby Mole, David Bentley, Pat Diggs, and Chris Whittington.

For his wise counsel in work and life, I thank my representative Richard Leibner. For his early and enduring belief in my writing career, I thank Raphael Sagalyn.

I need to credit those who've reviewed the manuscript for *The Hardball Handbook*—my wife, Kathleen; Tina Urbanski; Jeremy Bronson; Brooke Brower; author Jon Meacham; and, especially, my friend the esteemed editor Michele Slung. I want to credit *The Oxford Book of Aphorisms*; *Words of Wisdom* by William Safire and Leonard Safir; *The Yale Book of Quotations*; and *The Routledge Book of World Proverbs* for some of the epigraphs that introduce the chapters.

And now for my big thanks to editor Susan Mercandetti of Random House, who invested herself in this book, imagined and guided the project from the outset, and both pushed and pulled me to the final product. It was Susan who laid out the entire course traveled by *The Hardball Handbook* from the first to the final draft. I need to thank, as well, her colleagues at Random House: Jonathan Jao, Gina Centrello, Tom Perry, London King, Karen Fink, Janet Wygal, and Carole Lowenstein.

As with television, bringing a book to its audience is a team effort. While Hemingway is right that we must spend our lives to learn the simplest things, it is only with the help of others that we make something of them.

Index

administrative assistants (AAs)
  CM as, 23, 27, 30, 37
  obtaining meetings with, 6, 9–10
  successor to Wayne Owens, 27,
    28–29
  Wayne Owens as, 9–10, 12
Ailes, Roger
  hired by NBC to run CNBC and
    America's Talking networks,
    38–39
  as media guru, 38, 123
Allen, George, 112–13
Allen, Woody, 72
Alter, Jonathan, 142
Antisthenes, 26
Atwater, Lee, 129, 163

Baker, Jim, 70, 72, 84, 90–92
Begala, Paul, 107

Bentsen, Lloyd, 116–17
Berra, Yogi, 73
Biden, Joseph, 146–47
Blythe, Bill, 16
Boland, Eddie, 33
Boxer, Barbara, 34
Bradlee, Ben, 141
Brady, James, 173
Brothers, Joyce, 40
Buckley, William F., 175
Bush, Barbara, 47
Bush, George H.W.
  in 1988 presidential campaign,
    158, 162–63
  admission of ineloquence, 158
  career experience, 67–68
  as diplomat and politician,
    67–72
  hosts two generations of
    Matthews family, 46–47

Bush, George H.W. (*cont'd*):
  investments in people, 68–72
  and Jim Baker, 91
  as listener, 46, 47
  on opening day of 1989 baseball
    season, 70
Bush, George W.
  in 2000 presidential campaign,
    109
  in 2004 reelection campaign,
    44–45, 57
  and Dick Cheney, 93–94
  failure to lowball, 153–54
  fires Rumsfeld, 97
  and Hurricane Katrina, 43
  and "Mission Accomplished"
    banner, 153–54
  old DUI story, 156–57
  at World Trade Center after
    9/11, 43
Bush, Laura, 109

campaigning, defined, 22–23
Cannon, Joe, 103
Capitol Hill News Service, 130
Capitol police, 10–12, 15
Capone, Al, 12
Capra, Frank, 120
Carter, Jimmy
  in 1976 presidential campaign,
    63–64, 188
  in 1980 reelection campaign,
    51–52, 63, 97, 123–24
  CM as speechwriter for, 13, 26,
    37, 88, 90, 178
  and Jerry Rafshoon, 105
  "malaise" speech and aftermath,
    50–51
Carville, James, 162
Casey, Bob, 181–84
CBS News, 38
Cheney, Dick
  in 2004 reelection campaign, 57
  career summary, 93

  in Ford administration, 36
  hunting accident, 155–56
  as vice president, 93–94
Chesterfield, Lord, 40
The Chris Matthews Show (TV
    show), 4, 26, 45, 101, 175,
    176
Churchill, Winston
  bitten by political bug, 184–85
  early exploits, 139–40
  and FDR, 56, 94
  as hero of JFK, 171, 172
  postwar views, 171–72
  quotes, 79, 139, 150, 160, 176
  as role model, 174
Cleveland, Grover, 108
Clifford, Clark, 94, 187
Clinton, Bill
  in 1974 Arkansas congressional
    race, 18–19, 21
  in 1992 New Hampshire
    primary, 17–18, 19, 20
  in 1992 presidential campaign,
    162
  during 1995 government
    shutdown, 21
  boyhood, 16–17
  as Comeback Kid, 19–20
  dealing with skeletons, 162–63
  and draft letter, 17–18
  elected governor of Arkansas,
    19
  at Georgetown University, 18,
    41, 117–18
  and Lewinsky scandal, 20,
    99–100, 101, 109
  as listener, 40–41
  and Machiavelli, 43
  as optimist, 57
  as Rhodes scholar, 40
Clinton, Hillary
  in 2008 presidential campaign,
    59, 109–10
  as listener, 41–42
  listening tour, 42

as New York candidate for
U.S. Senate seat,
41–42
response to criticism of her,
21–22, 160–62
Clinton, Roger, 17
CNBC, 38, 39
Code of the Secret Service
(movie), 173, 174
Cohn, Roy, 148
Colson, Charles, 99
Corvo, David, 38
Cuban Missile Crisis, 172
Culhane, Hank, 152
Cunningham, Kathleen, *see*
Matthews, Kathleen
Cunningham
Cuomo, Mario, 57

Dean, Howard, 99
Delahanty, Thomas, 173
Dellums, Ron, 34
Democratic National Committee,
37, 62, 63
Dewey, Thomas, 114–15
Diehl, Leo, 34
Disraeli, Benjamin, 49
Dole, Robert, 116
Donaldson, Sam, 132
Douglas, Helen Gahagan,
153
Dreams from My Father (book),
54
Dukakis, Michael, 162–63

Eagleton, Thomas, 98
Early, Joe, 33
Eden, Anthony, 185
Edwards, John, 57, 160–61
Ehrlichman, John, 99
Eilberg, Joshua, 130
Ephron, Nora, 158
Epicurus, 31

Fala (Roosevelt's dog), 121–22
Feinstein, Dianne, 142–43
Firing Line (TV show), 175
Flaherty, Pete, 183
Fleetwood Mac, 57
Flowers, Gennifer, 18
Ford, Gerald, 91, 99
Fox, Michael J., 124–25
Fox News, 39
Franklin, Benjamin, 187
Franks, Marty, 37
Friedersdorf, Max, 84–85

Geffen, David, 161
General Electric Theater, 106, 173
Gephardt, Richard, 46
Gillespie, Ed, 62–63
Gingrich, Newt, 21, 134–35
Gipp, George, 106
Giuliani, Rudolph, 73–74,
110–11
Gold, Vic, 70
Goldwater, Barry, 106
Gonzales, Alberto, 98
Gorbachev, Mikhail, 39
Gore, Al, 109, 160, 188–89
Gregg, Allen, 188
Griffin, Bob, 33

Haddad, Tammy, 81, 177
Haldeman, Bob, 99
Hardball (book), 22
Hardball (TV show), 4, 26, 39,
79, 82, 83, 101, 113, 161,
175, 176, 189
Hart, Gary, 32–33, 99
Hearst, Will, 149, 150
Heinz, John, 107
Henry V, king of England, 121
Hertzberg, Hendrik, 36–37
Hinckley, John, 173, 174
Hirohito, Emperor, 69
Hopkins, Harry, 94

Horton, Willie, 162
Hurricane Katrina, 43

Iraq War
  "Mission Accomplished"
    banner, 153–54
  treatment of wounded soldiers,
    75

Jacobs, Eli, 70
Jefferson, Thomas, 112, 118
Johnson, Lyndon, 7, 115

Kaifu, Toshiki, 69, 71
Kaplan, Rick, 81
Kasich, John, 34
Katrina, Hurricane, 43
Kennedy, Edward "Ted"
  in 1980 presidential campaign,
    97
  campaigns for Wayne Owens in
    1972, 152
  as optimist, 58
  Wayne Owens as aide to, 9
Kennedy, John F.
  in 1960 presidential campaign,
    5, 13, 86, 97, 106
  and Bay of Pigs invasion,
    157–58
  Churchill as hero, 171–72
  and Clark Clifford, 94–95
  as congressman, 24
  covers founding U.N.
    conference, 55–56
  creates Peace Corps, 5
  and Cuban Missile Crisis, 172
  first campaign for Congress, 63
  funeral, 12
  historic mission, 188
  vs. Nixon, 86, 106
  as optimist, 56

and Pierre Salinger, 146
  and PT-109 heroism, 79,
    140–41
  Quayle compares himself to,
    116–17
  quotes, 171, 181
Kennedy, Robert F., 9, 16, 146,
  158
Kerrey, Bob, 99
Kerry, John
  in 2004 presidential campaign,
    3, 42–44, 45, 57, 80,
    164–67
  fails to respond to Swift Boat
    attacks, 164–67
  perceived as downbeat in
    2004 presidential campaign,
    57
  as talker, not listener, 43–44,
    45
Kilpatrick, James J., 37
Kipling, Rudyard, 137
Kissinger, Henry, 155
Kohl, Helmut, 68
Kramer, Larry, 37–38

La Guardia, Fiorello, 157
Lawrence, David, 182
Leaming, Barbara, 172
legislative assistants (LAs)
  CM in Frank Moss's office,
    12–13, 26, 27–29
  as early CM job goal, 5–6
  first offer, 7–8, 9
Leno, Jay, 177
Lewinsky scandal, 20, 99–100,
  101, 109
Limbaugh, Rush, 125
Lincoln, Abraham, 185–86, 188
listening, importance of, 40–48
Longfellow, Henry Wadsworth, 3
Longworth, Alice Roosevelt,
  168

Lott, Trent, 135
lowball principle, 152–53

Machiavelli, Niccolò
  being on the spot, 42–43
  need for prince to be
    questioner, 94
  quotes, 59, 171
  view of contributions, 59, 61
  and White House layout, 90
Mackay, Harvey, 67
Maraniss, David, 41, 117
Markey, Edward, 119–21
Matthews, Caroline, 45
Matthews, Chris
  as assistant to Rep. Tip O'Neill,
    13–14, 23–24, 26, 27, 30,
    33, 37, 147, 177
  becomes columnist for *San
    Francisco Examiner,* 37–38
  becomes Washington bureau
    chief for *San Francisco
    Examiner,* 38, 149–50
  as Capitol policeman, 10–12,
    15, 27, 177–78
  career summary, 26–27
  on Carter's White House staff,
    13, 26, 36–37, 88, 90, 178
  and *The Chris Matthews Show,*
    4, 26, 45, 101, 175, 176
  becomes legislative assistant, 26
  Democratic Party affiliation, 47
  as grad student at University of
    North Carolina, 37, 176
  and *Hardball,* 4, 26, 39, 79,
    82, 83, 101, 113, 161, 175,
    176, 189
  as AA to O'Neill, 27, 30, 37
  heroes, 174–75
  initial job search on Capitol
    Hill, 5–10
  as legislative assistant to Sen.
    Frank Moss, 12–13, 26, 27–29

  as long shot candidate for
    Congress, 129–32
  as newspaperman, 26, 37–38,
    149–50
  on-air bout with Zell Miller,
    79–83
  in Peace Corps, 5, 9, 11, 143,
    177
  on Senate Budget Committee,
    26, 29
  as speechwriter, 13, 26, 30, 37,
    88, 90, 177–79
  as speechwriter for Pres. Jimmy
    Carter, 88
  start of television career, 38
Matthews, Herb, 46–47, 129
Matthews, Jim, 129
Matthews, Kathleen
    Cunningham, 37, 51
Matthews, Mary, 31, 46–47
Matthews, Michael, 17
McAuliffe, Terry, 62, 63
McCain, John
  in 2008 presidential campaign,
    60, 119
  as prisoner of war, 137–38
McCarthy, Eugene, 181
McCarthy, Joe, 148
McCarthy, Timothy, 173
McCaskill, Claire, 124–25
McGinniss, Joe, 38, 174
McGovern, George, 28, 33, 98
McGraw, Tug, 49
The McLaughlin Group (TV
    show), 175
Milk, Harvey, 142
Miller, George, 34
Miller, Zell, 3–4, 79–83
mission, importance of, 189–90
Mitterand, François, 71
Mondale, Walter, 32, 124
Monicagate, 20, 99–100, 101,
    109
Moscone, George, 142

Moss, Frank
background, 9
CM as legislative assistant to,
12–13, 26, 27–28, 29
CM as speechwriter, 11, 177–78
CM's initial work for, 10, 11,
177–78
as mentor to CM, 98, 131–32
Moynihan, Daniel Patrick, 41, 88
MSNBC cable network
2004 Republican National
Convention coverage, 3–4,
79–83
America's Talking as fore-
runner, 38
Hardball show, 4, 26, 39, 79,
82, 83, 101, 113, 161, 175,
176, 189
Mubarak, Hosni, 69, 70, 71
Murtha, Jack, 31, 32, 34
Muskie, Edmund, 29, 187–88,
189

Nader, Ralph, 130
New Orleans, La., 43
Nixon, Richard
in 1950 Senate campaign,
153
in 1960 presidential campaign,
13, 86, 106
in 1968 presidential campaign,
38
in 1972 reelection campaign,
98
farewell White House speech,
86–87
vs. Kennedy, 86, 106
and ten-second rule, 115
and Watergate, 99, 101

Obama, Barack
at 2004 Democratic National
Convention, 52–54

in 2008 presidential campaign,
xiii, 21, 49, 59–60, 110,
147–48
autobiography, 54
backer David Geffen, 161
O'Donnell, Kirk, 87
O'Neill, Kip, 35
O'Neill, Thomas P. "Tip"
CM as assistant to, 13–14,
23–24, 26, 27, 30, 33, 37,
147, 177
first political campaign, 65
as listener, 46
and Newt Gingrich, 134–35
power of speakership, 108–9
relationship with Reagan, 13,
23, 24, 39, 83–85, 92,
132–33
"snow button" story, 32
as Speaker of the House, 23–24
success by association concept,
147
view of loyalty, 32–33, 39
optimism, 52–58
Owens, Wayne
in 1968 Bobby Kennedy
campaign, 9, 146
1972 run for Congress, 9, 27,
28, 75, 152
as administrative assistant to
Frank Moss, 9–10, 12
best career advice, 146

Paar, Jerry, 173–74
Panetta, Leon, 34
Peace Corps
CM in, 5, 9, 11, 143, 177
signing of authorization bill, 7
Pelosi, Nancy
CM's view, 14, 150–52
as first woman elected
Speaker of the House, 14,
31–32
and lowball principle, 152

supports Jack Murtha for House
Majority Leader, 31–32
Pettigrew, Richard, 36
Plowden, Pamela, 184
politicians
asking for campaign
contributions, 59–66
bitten by bug, 181–86
campaigning, defined, 22–23
Congress as clubhouse world,
33–35
exceeding expectations, 150–54
and friendship, 33, 35–36, 39
getting bad news out, 155–59
group photo tips, 145
knowing where power lies,
88–95
as listeners, 40–48
and loyalty, 28, 32–33, 36, 39,
63, 88
and optimism, 52–58
protecting reputation, 165–68
staying in touch, 73–76
ten-second rule, 113–18
Politics (TV show), 39
Powers, Dave, 97

Quayle, Dan, 116–17

Rafshoon, Jerry, 105
Reagan, Nancy, 55, 91
Reagan, Ronald
in 1980 presidential campaign,
37, 52, 119, 123–24
at 1981 inauguration
ceremony, 173
in 1984 reelection campaign,
123–24
as actor, 174
assassination attempt, 173–74
bear anecdote, 96–97
comeback after assassination
attempt, 55

FDR as hero, 172–73
as *GE Theater* host, 106, 173
as Great Communicator, 13,
23, 24
historic mission, 188
and Jim Baker, 91–93
and Margaret Thatcher, 68
as optimist, 52, 56–57
performance on TV, 106–7
personality, 97
political advice, 104, 106–7
quotes, 79, 119
relationship with Tip O'Neill,
13, 23, 24, 39, 83–85, 92,
132–33
respect for FDR, 172–73
"there you go again" remark,
119, 123
unlikely friendships, 39, 79,
83–85, 92, 132–33
Reid, Harry, 104–5
Republican National Committee,
62–63
Republican National Convention
(1988), 158
Republican National Convention
(2004), 3–4, 79–83, 110
reputations, protecting, 165–68
rivalries, 30
Rockefeller, Nelson, 98
Romney, George, 98
Romney, Mitt, 59
Roosevelt, Eleanor, 141
Roosevelt, Franklin Delano
and Fala, 121–22
and Harry Hopkins, 94
as hero of Reagan's, 172–73
historic mission, 188
as optimist, 56
polio as testing moment,
141–42
Roosevelt, Theodore
early exploits, 137, 138–39, 140
quotes, 103, 137
as warrior, 137, 138–39

Roth, Hyman, 21
Rumsfeld, Donald, 36, 97

Sadat, Anwar, 69
Safire, William, 112
Salinger, Pierre, 146
San Francisco Chronicle, 26
San Francisco Examiner, 26,
    37–38, 149
Saturday Night Live, 189
Schwarzenegger, Arnold, 83,
    103–4, 167–68
Schwarzkopf, Norman, 152
Secret Service, 173–74
The Selling of the President 1968
    (book), 38, 174
Senate Budget Committee, 26,
    29
September 11 attacks, 43, 73
Sevareid, Eric, 175
Sidarth, S.R., 112–13
Simpson, O.J., 39
Sinatra, Frank, 56
60 Minutes, 162
Sorensen, Ted, 5, 7, 13, 64, 174
Sorenson, Rich, 132
Spalding, Chuck, 55–56
Specter, Arlen, 184
speeches, six-step system,
    178–80
Stalin, Joseph, 171–72
Stein, Ben, 3
Stengel, Casey, 129
Stephanopoulos, George,
    162–63
Stringer, Howard, 38
Swift Boat Veterans for Truth,
    164

Talent, Jim, 124
Tate, James H.J., 182
Taylor, Leroy, 11

Teeley, Peter, 68–69, 71
ten-second rule, 113–18
Thatcher, Margaret, 68, 71
The Third Man (movie), 96
Thornburgh, Richard, 107
The Tonight Show (TV show), 177
Towne, Henson, 75–76
Truman, Harry, 94, 122–23, 187
Trump, Donald, 22
Tsongas, Paul, 19
Tuck, Dick, 16, 153
TV Guide, 82
Twain, Mark, 187

Vidal, Gore, 96

Walker, Bob, 134–35
Walter Reed Army Medical
    Center, 75
war room, 162, 163, 168
Warner, John, 45
Washington, George, 145
Watergate, 99, 101
Wells, H.G., 59
The West Wing (TV show), 88,
    89, 90
White House
    CM on Carter's staff, 13, 26,
        30, 36–37, 88, 90, 178
    Nixon's farewell speech, 86–87
    what it's like to work there,
        88–90
Whittington, Harry, 156
Will, George F., 175
Williams, Edward Bennett, 70
Williams, Ted, 70
Winfrey, Oprah, 48
Wofford, Harris, 107–8
Wolfson, Howard, 161
World Trade Center, 43, 73
Wright, (Reverend) Jeremiah,
    147–48

ABOUT THE AUTHOR

CHRIS MATTHEWS is best known as the host of *Hardball* and *The Chris Matthews Show*. He has distinguished himself as a broadcast journalist, newspaper bureau chief, presidential speechwriter, and bestselling author. He covered the fall of the Berlin Wall, the first all-races election in South Africa, the Good Friday Peace Accord in Northern Ireland, and the funeral of Pope John Paul II, as well as every American presidential election campaign since 1980.

Matthews has received the David Brinkley Award for Excellence in Broadcast Journalism and the Gold Medal Award from the Pennsylvania Society. He was a visiting fellow at Harvard University's John F. Kennedy Institute of Politics. He holds twenty-one honorary degrees.

Matthews worked for fifteen years as a newspaper journalist, thirteen of them as Washington bureau chief for the *San Francisco Examiner* and two as a national columnist for the *San Francisco Chronicle*.

Matthews worked in the U.S. Senate for five years for Senator Frank Moss of Utah and Senator Edmund Muskie of Maine; in the White House for four years under President Jimmy Carter as a presidential speechwriter and on the Presidential Reorganization Project; then for six years as the top aide to Speaker of the House Thomas P. "Tip" O'Neill, Jr.

He is married to Kathleen Matthews, executive vice president of Marriott International. They have three children: Michael, Thomas, and Caroline.

ABOUT THE TYPE

This book was set in Fairfield, the first typeface from the hand of the distinguished American artist and engraver Rudolph Ruzicka (1883–1978). Ruzicka was born in Bohemia and came to America in 1894. He set up his own shop, devoted to wood engraving and printing, in New York in 1913 after a varied career working as a wood engraver, in photoengraving and banknote printing plants, and as an art director and freelance artist. He designed and illustrated many books, and was the creator of a considerable list of individual prints—wood engravings, line engravings on copper, and aquatints.